PREACHING
PROVERBS

PREACHING PROVERBS

Wisdom for the Pulpit

ALYCE M. MCKENZIE

Westminster John Knox Press
Louisville, Kentucky

Scripture quotations from the New Revised Standard Version of the Bible are copyright © 1989 by the Division of Christian Education of the National Council of the Churches of Christ in the U.S.A. and are used by permission.

Acknowledgments appear on page x.

Book design by Jennifer K. Cox
Cover design by Kim Wohlenhaus
Cover art is a detail from the painting titled Proverbidioms ' *T. E. Breitenbach 1975. For a catalog of posters write: T. E. Breitenbach, Altamont, NY 12009-0538.*

First edition

Published by Westminster John Knox Press
Louisville, Kentucky

This book is printed on acid-free paper that meets the American National Standards Institute Z39.48 standard. ⊗

PRINTED IN THE UNITED STATES OF AMERICA

96 97 98 99 00 01 02 03 04 05 — 10 9 8 7 6 5 4 3 2 1

Library of Congress Cataloging-in-Publication Data
McKenzie, Alyce M., date.
    Preaching proverbs : wisdom for the pulpit / Alyce M. McKenzie — 1st ed.
      p.   cm.
    Includes bibliographical references and index.
    ISBN 0-664-25653-8 (alk. paper)
    1. Bible—Proverbs.   2. Bible—Homiletical use.   3. Bible. O.T. Proverbs—Homiletical use.   4. Bible. N.T. Gospels—Homiletical use.   5. Jesus Christ—Sayings.   6. Bible. O.T. Ecclesiastes—Homiletical use.   I. Title.
BS680.P7M37   1996
251—dc20   96-17775

Contents

113932

Preface

In the last chapter of this book there is a sermon whose central metaphor is my almost tripping over a lost-and-found box on my way into church on Sunday mornings. It was a box filled with items crucial for daily living such as keys and reading glasses, and I had the urge to carry the box with me into church and walk up and down the aisles distributing these essential items to people squinting nearsightedly at their bulletins or locked out of their houses. That action could serve as a metaphor for this entire book, which is an attempt to distribute for daily use the crucial contents of a lost-and-found box, the proverbial wisdom of our biblical tradition. Chapters 8 and 9 set forth several sermons on proverbial texts for those who wish to see the homiletical benefits of retrieving proverbs for preaching.

This book had its beginnings the day, several years ago, when I arrived late to a graduate hermeneutics class. It was a bad day to be late, because the professor was in the act of assigning dates for participants to present major papers on the topic of relating a genre of biblical literature to contemporary life. Getting the last choice of dates naturally meant being the first to present a paper. Faced with a big task and less than two weeks' preparation time, I headed straight for the library, determined to find out which genre was most neglected in the scholarly literature. By far the shortest bibliography belonged to the proverb. A relationship that began with expediency quickly matured into genuine admiration. I began to appreciate biblical proverbs as a rich source of practical wisdom, capable of ethical guidance in the challenging situations of daily life. I began to recognize the proverbs of Jesus as the building blocks of a counter-view of life, over against what passes for wisdom in a violent, individualistic, acquisitive culture. With my newfound alertness to proverbs on the cultural airwaves, I began to realize that secular consumer marketing, with its goal of life as continual acquisition of material luxuries, is better at keeping its proverbial wisdom before the people than are we Christian preachers. Biblical proverbial wisdom from both the Hebrew scriptures and the New Testament, a rich resource for forming group identity in and over against the culture, was being bypassed in the pulpit. (My use of the term Hebrew scriptures acknowledges that not all of this biblical material was composed in Hebrew. I have chosen it as the least cumbersome way of referring to that body of writings which are both the scriptures of the community of Israel and the first testament of the Christian Bible.)

The more I came to appreciate proverbs, the more I became convinced that proverbs need to be called forth from the tomb into a pulpit resurrection. They languish, bound in graveclothes of misconceptions about their identity and function. One misconception is that they are self-evident moralisms. When this is stripped away, we find that in reality they are ethical insights born out of specific situations, and that their rhetorical desire is to be used as spotlights to illuminate certain contemporary scenarios. Another misguided notion is that the only function of proverbs is to serve as propaganda for the status quo. In reality, they can also function to subvert it, as evidenced by the sayings of Qohelet (the sage who collected the sayings in the book of Ecclesiastes), the proverbs of the Synoptic Jesus, and many contemporary sayings as well. Biblical and contemporary proverbs share the same structure and functions and can therefore be put side by side in sermons, in conflict or conversation, to shape the identity of communities of faith in relation to their cultural milieus.

Part One introduces proverbs as wisdom for the pulpit. Chapter 1 sets forth the proverb's syntax, structure, and cultural functions, helping the preacher to identify the proverb in scripture and in contemporary life. Chapter 2 deals with how proverbs function in our culture as well as in the Bible. It counters the prevailing view that proverbs are only capable of inculcating traditional virtues, drawing on their subversive use by Qohelet and the Synoptic Jesus. Chapter 3 sets out a method for allowing proverbs to shape sermons that tap their capacity to both create and subvert order. It employs reader-response theory's notion of *defamiliarization:* that profound literary communication makes readers' habitual assumptions seem strange to them.

Part Two describes proverbs that create and subvert order in scripture and today. Chapter 4 examines proverbs from the book of Proverbs that create order, encouraging traditional virtues conducive to community stability. Chapter 5 looks at proverbs that subvert order, from Qohelet, and chapter 6 deals with those of the Synoptic

Jesus. Chapter 7 is a sampler of contemporary proverbs that create and subvert order.

Part Three consists of sermon models for preaching proverbs that create and subvert order. Chapter 8 offers three models for preaching on proverbs that create order: the "Roving Spotlight" model, the "Sometimes, but Not Always" model, and the "Double Take" model. Chapter 9 offers three basic models for preaching proverbs of counter-order, primarily from the New Testament, but also from the Hebrew Scriptures: the "Dueling Proverbs" model, the "Challenger" model, and the "Advocate" model.

Many colleagues, friends, and family members contributed to the process of writing this project. I want to thank Thomas G. Long, friend and mentor, for his own insightful work on proverbs as well as his encouragement and wise direction in this project. I am indebted to Choon-Leong Seow, who first pointed me toward the subversive nature of Qohelet's sentence wisdom, and who offered invaluable suggestions for shaping the chapters on Proverbs and Qohelet.

Scott Black Johnston, Eugene L. Lowry, and Christine M. Smith provided important suggestions on various chapters. Wolfgang Mieder's extensive writings about contemporary American proverbs have proved invaluable in my research. So have his enthusiasm about the project and his comments on the chapter on contemporary proverbs. I wish to thank Timothy Staveteig, acquisitions editor at Westminster John Knox, for believing in the project from the very beginning and for his suggestions for making the book more accessible to readers. Marci A. Hamilton, professor of law at Benjamin N. Cardoza School of Law, has contributed not only her friendship but also her expertise in legal hermeneutics, helping me to view my analysis of reader-response criticism from an interdisciplinary perspective. My colleagues in various forums at Princeton Theological Seminary and the Academy of Homiletics have made helpful comments on the text, and the congregations of Yardley United Methodist Church, Harriman United Methodist Church, and Neshamony United Methodist Church have been gracious participants in services of worship in which proverbs were preached. My parents and extended family has provided interest and encouragement. My children, Melissa, Rebecca, and Matthew, have called forth wisdom from me and taught it to me as well. A special thanks to my husband, Murry, for his unquenchable optimism and humor about life in general and this project in particular.

Acknowledgments

Grateful acknowledgment is made to the following for permission to reproduce copyrighted material.

Abingdon Press, for excerpts from *Soul Theology,* by Henry H. Mitchell and Nicholas Cooper Lewter. Copyright © 1986 by Henry H. Mitchell and Nicholas Cooper Lewter. Reprinted by permission of the publisher, Abingdon Press.

Daughters of Sarah, for excerpt from Vivian Elaine Johnson, "Little Brother," from the spring 1995 issue.

HarperCollins Publishers, Inc., for excerpts from *Upon This Book: The Miracles of a Black Church,* by Samuel G. Freedman (1993).

Huntingdon House Publishers, for excerpts from Steve Arrington, *Journey into Darkness: Nowhere to Land* (1992).

Lifeline, for permission to paraphrase portions of Barbara Walter's 1978 television interview with Burt Reynolds.

The Philadelphia Inquirer, for quotations from David O'Reilly, "Converting the Klansman" (April 1995); Monica Rhor, "Giving a lift to voices and hope in an oft songless city" (July 29, 1995); and Carlin Romano, "A daughter of Florida" (February 19, 1995).

Weavings: A Journal of the Christian Spiritual Life, for excerpts from Judith C. MacNutt, "How I Discovered Inner Healing," in vol. 6, no. 4 (July–August 1991), and Stephen V. Doughty, "Glimpsing Glimpses: A Quest for Communal Discernment," in vol. 10, no. 6 (November–December 1995). Copyright 1991 and 1995 by The Upper Room.

Introduction
The Preacher as Sage

Most preachers, as well as most lectionaries, avoid biblical proverbs, preferring instead more familiar and accessible lessons from psalms and epistles or the Gospel narratives and parables. But while pastors are in their studies skipping right past proverbs on the way to somewhere else, their congregations are out in the world living by proverbs. Imagine a pastor who, after a morning working on Sunday's sermon, gets into her car to make pastoral visits. Her mind is busy reflecting on the preacher's perennial question: How can I put the biblical witness into faithful, engaging conversation with the worldview and needs of my parishioners?

Pondering this large question, she turns on the radio, which happens to be tuned to the local country station. Her ears are greeted by the dulcet refrain "You've got to stand for something or you'll fall for anything." Driving along the highway, her mind engaged in textual and congregational analysis, she passes a billboard that depicts a gigantic three-dimensional sneaker with the words "Just do it!" Above the bed of her parishioner at the nursing center is a poster depicting a brightly colored flowering plant with the caption "Bloom where you are planted." Her next stop is the welfare office, where she is to meet a parishioner in need of help in clarifying her benefits. On the way to the caseworker's desk, she walks past a poster tacked on the bulletin board showing a child standing at a crossroads and bearing as its caption the Korean proverb "A journey of a thousand miles begins with one step."

As our first pastor is making her rounds, another pastor is attending a church growth seminar, with participants sitting around a flip chart brainstorming alternatives to "doing church." Says the leader, "Many late-twentieth-century Americans are technologically sophisticated; they love informality; they crave experiences of faith. How do we honor those skills and desires without compromising the gospel in our preaching and worship?" Several participants in the seminar raise questions: "Where does a legitimate use of aspects of contemporary cultural life shade into inappropriate accommodation to the culture? How can I put the popular wisdom of my people in conversation with the biblical witness?"

The seminar adjourns, and, still ruminating on these issues, our second pastor sets off on a round of errands. At the mall, he stops for a soda at a frozen-yogurt stand. "I'd like a Sprite," he informs the clerk. "No problem!" the clerk comforts him cheerily. Then, as he dispenses the change, the clerk also dispenses the blessing that has become a contemporary command: "Have a nice day!" Feeling vaguely resentful at being told what to do with his day, our second pastor walks on, pondering how he is going to lead a trustees meeting that night. A local synagogue's Hebrew school has asked permission to rent the use of several of the rooms in his church's new building addition one night a week. "Is this really how Jesus would want us to use our new building?" one of the trustees had asked at last month's meeting. Tonight would be the vote.

With visions of conflict dancing in his head, our pastor walks by a retail store called "Successories," a company that specializes in products to help companies and individuals set goals and improve performance and motivation. If he were to go in, he would find shelf after shelf of books, greeting cards, stationery, T-shirts (referred to as "attitude apparel"), wall plaques, posters, calendars, paperweights, and coffee mugs bearing contemporary inspirational proverbial sayings. He would find audiotapes of contemporary motivational workshops in which upbeat proverbs figure prominently. On the walls he would see row after row of shiny plaques engraved with inspirational sayings on themes of risk taking, leadership, teamwork, goal setting, determination, and attitude. He stops for a moment, his eye caught by the bright colors in the display window. It features two posters. One is of a ship on a stormy sea, with the caption "Anyone can hold the helm when the sea is calm." A second pictures an adult's hand holding a child's hand, and it reads "We make a living by what we get. We make a life by what we give." "I can't believe people really buy this stuff," he mutters to himself, shaking his head at the large number of people milling around the aisles, and walks on.

His next stop is the real estate office where he has an appointment to talk with a realtor about finding warehouse space to rent for his church's burgeoning food and clothing pantry. He barely notices the sign over the agent's desk that says, "Everybody has his price." Then it's on to the high school for a conference about his daughter. On her history teacher's desk is a notice printed in such big letters he can't miss it. "Lack of planning on your part does not constitute an emergency on my part." His mind wandering for a moment, he contrasts it with the sign she has hanging on her bedroom wall: "Clean up the planet but not my room!" and briefly wonders what would happen if the two signs were switched.

An inner-city pastor is meanwhile counseling a parishioner depressed because of circumstances that dictate he must go to college half time rather than full time. "The race is not always to the swift," says the pastor. At the covered-dish supper that night, he overhears a snippet of a conversation as he moves around greeting his people. "Different strokes for different folks, I guess," says a woman, shaking her head over the behavior of a neighbor. After supper, the congregation gathers to sing "Through many dangers, toils, and snares, I have already come," and nobody needs to look down at the hymnal to remember the next line, "'Tis grace hath brought me safe thus far, and grace will lead me home."

PROVERBS EVERYWHERE BUT THE PULPIT

Preoccupied with pondering the sermon for the week, we most often pass by proverbs with unseeing eyes and upturned noses. We walk and drive by them on billboards, T-shirts, coffee mugs, cartoons, magazine ads, bumper stickers, and posters. Busy reflecting on how we can put biblical wisdom in conversation with contemporary wisdom, we hear them with unlistening ears, as the refrains of songs, in media commercials, and in conversations. Proverbs! Constantly used by the people, consistently ignored by many preachers. Proverbs, which have been found almost everywhere in the world and in almost every period in human history. Proverbs, which continue to be used and coined in various cultures throughout the world today, including our own.

Not only do proverbs season secular discourse; they pepper the Bible as well. They appear in the historical and prophetic books, Proverbs, Job, Ecclesiastes, the Synoptic sayings attributed to Jesus, the letters of Paul, and the Gospel of John. Familiar examples include "Better is a dry morsel with quiet than a house full of feasting with strife" (Prov. 17:1). "For everything there is a season, and a time for every matter under heaven" (Eccl. 3:1). "One does not live by bread alone" (Luke 4:4). "It is not what goes into the mouth that defiles a person, but it is what comes out of the mouth that defiles" (Matt. 15:11).

About the only place proverbs do not seem to be found today is in the pulpit. That is cause for community lament, because proverbs, both biblical and cultural, are some of the most useful tools a community has for self-analysis, ethical direction, and identity formation. Proverbs reveal the essential character of the people who collect and use them. Contemporary cultural proverbs show us the shape we are currently in and the shape of things to come, while biblical proverbs are capable of shaping the identity of the people of God. Clearly, Americans have an appetite for popular wisdom couched in proverbial terms. This makes it crucial for preachers to turn to biblical proverbs to set the prevailing common wisdom in theological context, at times confirming it, at other times challenging its distortions. As Thomas G. Long points out, "The question is not will people live by proverbs, but what kind of proverbs will they cherish?"[1] Or, more pointedly, by whose proverbs will they live? The answer, in large part, depends on the contemporary preacher!

A FAVORABLE CLIMATE
FOR PROVERB APPRECIATION

The time is ripe for the pulpit resuscitation of the proverb, given recent developments in the understanding of preaching. Whereas topical preaching reigned during the 1960s and 1970s, the past twenty years or so have seen a resurgence of the traditional recognition that distinctively Christian preaching is biblical preaching. At the same time, there has been an increase in lectionary use, encouraged by the liturgical renewal movement, which has helped to ground biblical preaching in contemporary liturgical practice. Biblical preaching does not refer to a sermon that is sprinkled with an ample number of biblical quotations. Rather, biblical preaching refers to sermons that engage a particular biblical text or texts in dialogue with a particular community of faith.

An invaluable subtype of biblical preaching has stepped boldly into the homiletical spotlight in recent years, genre-sensitive preaching. By that is meant preaching that allows itself to be shaped by the literary genres of the Bible. Such preaching views these genres as groupings of materials that share common rhetorical strategies. These strategies seek to involve readers at the levels of emotions and behavior as well as the cognition that has dominated traditional three-point sermon forms. Genre-sensitive preaching seeks to craft sermons that reflect these rhetorical strategies, shaping the interaction between sermon and hearers to the contours of the prior interaction between preacher and text.

For the most part, the genre of narrative has held center stage among advocates of genre-sensitive preaching, as it has in the fields of literary criticism, law, biblical studies, and ethics. To its credit, narrative has given many good homiletical performances without letting its fame go to its head. In fact, narrative shows every sign of a homiletical future of many happy returns. The problem is that while narrative basks in the spotlight, another insightful genre languishes in the wings. That genre is narrative's cousin, the proverbial genre, more diminutive in size, but every bit narrative's equal in potential helpfulness to the people in the pews.

Narratives seek to invite hearers and readers into a sweeping story line, seeing their lives in its story and situating the story in the midst of their lives. Proverbs arise out of sages' observing story lines going on around them and noting recurring patterns in those story lines. The proverb condenses a pattern into a partial generalization that expresses one way of interpreting these recurring situations. For this reason a proverb has been called "a short sentence founded upon long experience, containing a truth."[2]

The sages of Israel, observing recurring stories of individuals in verbal combat with one another, devised the proverbs "A soft answer turns away wrath, but a harsh word stirs up anger"(Prov. 15:1), and "Like somebody who takes a passing dog by the ears is one who meddles in the quarrel of another" (Prov. 26:17). These proverbs have obviously arisen out of anonymous sages' observation of narrative patterns in life around them. Far from being static statements of universal truth, proverbs make themselves available as wisdom tools for interpreting present and future life stories.

MISCONCEPTIONS ABOUT PROVERBS

One of the reasons for the lamentable underuse of the proverb in the contemporary pulpit is that preachers have not had a working definition of the distinctive structure and cultural function that make a proverb a proverb, whether biblical or contemporary. Lacking such a definition, they have made a couple of assumptions about proverbs that rob them of their relevance to specific contemporary situations. One misconception is that proverbs are general moralisms whose homiletical use is limited to topical dos-and-don'ts sermons on alcohol abuse, laziness, and the importance of honesty.

Another assumption that discourages preachers from attempting sermons on proverbs is the "coals to Newcastle" view of proverbs' pulpit usefulness. In this view, proverbs are so self-evident that there is no point in expounding their texts in sermons. At best they may be interspersed in sermons on other texts as memorable summaries of the preacher's points. While this is one use of proverbs in sermons, it is by no means the only one.

These misconceptions about the proverb's pulpit potential are based on a superficial understanding of the proverbial form. In reality, proverbs are "intricate literary expressions which are far more theological, less overtly moralistic, and more vitally related to lived experience than is apparent at first glance."[3] A proverb gains its ethical force not by being a universal moralism, but by seeking an "apt fit" with new situations. "The reader must perceive which constellation of experience is evoked by the proverb and which is not."[4] This process of discernment is the basic dynamic underlying all the models for preaching on proverbial texts offered in chapters 8 and 9.

A GENRE DEFINITION
THAT DOES PROVERBS JUSTICE

An understanding of the proverb's structure and cultural function acts as a lens through which preachers can spot proverbs throughout the biblical witness. Gazing through this lens, the preacher discerns that not everything in Proverbs is a proverb, and that many sayings in the New Testament not currently recognized as proverbial in form most certainly are. An understanding of the characteristics and capabilities of the proverbial genre also serves as a lens through which we can spot contemporary proverbs. It helps us to see that, while proverbs are a quintessentially oral genre, they still have an important function in literate cultures. Preachers, rather than dismissing proverbs as the arcane vestige of a preliterate day, need to recognize them as a germane rhetorical force in our people's present days. A definition of proverb structure and function helps us identify time-honored proverbs that form part of our collective American wisdom. It also helps us recognize those new proverbs which are continually being coined by groups within our culture.

Fresh proverbs are continually being minted. Several proverbs coined in this century are: "The grass is always greener on the other side of the fence," "Garbage in, garbage out" (a proverb coined by computer operators), "Different strokes for different folks," and "A woman's place is in the House and in the Senate."

The Proverb as Spotlight Not Floodlight

The proverb's unique contribution is this: that while it has arisen out of an originative situation, it transcends that situation to serve as an ethical spotlight on certain circumstances in contemporary life. A proverb is able, by virtue of its generalized syntax, vivid imagery, and present tense (or its equivalent), to make itself available beyond the situation of its origins to illuminate some, but not all, situations in the lives of contemporary hearers of sermons. From this context-transcending quality comes one of the most eloquent definitions of the proverb ever rendered: A proverb is "a winged word, outliving the fleeting moment."[5]

This quality is what William McKane cherishes as its "hermeneutical openness."[6] The wisdom of the proverb user determines which proverb fits which situation. Different people may use diametrically opposed proverbs to illuminate one and the same situation. This phenomenon is illustrated in a dialogue between two of Garrison Keillor's characters in his short story "Roy Bradley, Boy Broadcaster." Roy, a young man with aspirations to be a radio broadcaster, is still living at home, making ends meet by operating a roadside live-bait stand.

"When are you going to do something about radio?" his mother inquired in November.

"I have sent off dozens of applications. I'm waiting for word," he said, testily.

"You don't get anywhere waiting. Your father is proof of that."

"All things come to him who waits," he reminded her.

"God helps those who help themselves," she added.[7]

The clearest example of this in Proverbs is in 26:4, "Do not answer fools according to their folly, or you will be a fool yourself," which is immediately followed by "Answer fools according to their folly, or they will be wise in their own eyes"(26:5). Proverbs are partial generalizations, presenting interpretive options, not absolute or universal truths. They seek to be placed, by the wise decisions of contemporary sages, into specific story lines or situations in contemporary life. The proverb is a "risky rhetorical form," because "while it speaks wisdom, it also requires wisdom to be rightly heard and employed."[8] The burden falls on the wisdom of the preacher as sage to determine when a proverb is a "word fitly spoken . . . like apples of gold in a setting of silver" (25:11) and when that same proverb might be "a thornbush brandished by the hand of a drunkard" (26:9).

Proverbs have been underappreciated by preachers because the oral nature of proverbs can suffer when placed in literary collections. When found in a collection like Proverbs or in certain texts from the Synoptic Gospels, in catalogue fashion, largely stripped of interpretive clues, intermingled with admonitions and universal statements of truth, proverbs are easily mistaken by readers for moral absolutes. In such a collection, we easily lose sight of the proverb's unique capacity to illuminate a particular situation. The lectionary, in its egregious underrepresentation of proverbial texts from the Hebrew Scriptures, perpetuates the proverb's pulpit neglect by implying that such proverbs merely form a tiresome collection of self-evident moralisms.

The Proverb as Oral Genre in a Literate Culture

Another explanation for the conspicuous absence of proverbs, whether biblical or contemporary, from today's pulpits is the snobbery of a self-styled literate culture directed toward an oral genre. We Americans are heavy proverb users. Proverbs are frequently quoted in everyday conversation; they appear in dialogues in literary works and in popular songs; they are depicted in cartoons, and they are coined by contemporary philosophers. Their persuasive power is everywhere exploited by the advertising industry to sell us the particular brands of the things we genuinely need, as well as to portray luxuries as necessities.

While we use proverbs incessantly, we American often do so apologetically. This is because American culture tends to pride itself on its literacy, worshiping at the altar of literacy's high estimations of originality and individual authorship. Proverbs are not original to us, and we prefer dazzling people with our original verbal creations to quoting others, however wise. The most common objection to proverbs is that they have been so often repeated that they have lost their novelty. This is to confuse proverbs' time-honored, collective quality with triteness. This objection is itself trite, for it misses the point that the novelty and wisdom of proverbs are set free when they are used in new contexts of contemporary life. To use proverbs may well be to talk less and to say more.

Secondary Orality and the Recovery of the Proverb

The pervasive presence of proverbs in a culture that considers itself to be highly literate is proof that, even in literate cultures, oral forms continue to be used for their persuasive power. Tex Sample insists that pastors educated in the literate halls of academia wake up to the fact that many people both learn and express their faith in proverbs and stories. For preachers, this means a sensitivity to the proverbs and stories indigenous to local congregations in our worship, proclamation, teaching, and witness.[9] Sample is advocating a move toward what Leona Tubbs Tisdale calls "preaching as local theology and folk art," an intentional exegesis of congregational context in concert with biblical texts.[10] In fact, evidence is growing that our society is shifting from a literate to a postliterate or "secondary orality culture." For several centuries we have prized the memorable, formal, respectable qualities of written discourse. Now we are shifting to one that prefers communications that epitomize the colloquial, seemingly spontaneous character of oral communication.

The contemporary preference is for political campaign speeches that seem conversational and spontaneous rather than polished. Nielsen ratings outstrip book sales. More and more often, best-selling books are those that are reconstructed, under contract, from the screenplays of movies. Some linguists are convinced that, deep down, we are no longer a culture that values literacy.[11] Moral judgments on the shift aside, it makes the recovery of the oral genre of proverbs in preaching all the more timely and, indeed, crucial.

While preachers have not yet rediscovered the proverb, scholars from other quarters are beginning to give it the attention it deserves. Literary scholars are praising the proverb's aesthetic beauty, which is accomplished through rhyme, alliteration, repetition, and metaphor. Biblical scholars are lauding the proverb's ethically clarifying potential, when used in wise hands, as an interpretive tool in contemporary situations. Folklore scholars specializing in the proverb are giving it credit for the important role of cultural interpretation it played in biblical times as well as today. In folklorist Alan Dundes's terms, proverbs are uniquely equipped to convey the "folk ideas," basic premises, or cultural axioms that are the building blocks of the worldview of a group of people.[12]

The most common function of proverbs historically has been to inculcate the worldview of groups wielding power in a society. They have thereby come to be associated with traditional values, conservatism, and status quo preservation. This is the basic role they fulfill in the Proverbs collection, where they operate as tools of social control in the context of the tumultuous postexilic period. It is a mistake, however, to confuse proverbs' most common use with their inherent nature. In the hands of groups on the margins of social power and those who identify with them, proverbs become tools to subvert, not reinforce, traditional wisdom.

Contemporary proverbs can also subvert conventional wisdom. "A woman's place is in the House and in the Senate" subverts the misogynist wisdom of the earlier proverb "A woman's place is in the home." This subversive function of proverbs is what reader-response critic Wolfgang Iser calls *defamiliarization,* the capacity of profound literature to make people's habitual assumptions seem strange to them and therefore more open to critical analysis. His thought will be helpful to us in understanding proverbs' subversive potential in chapter 2.

Once the contemporary preacher comes to understand the linguistic and cultural properties of the proverb, he will be struck by an invaluable insight: that biblical proverbs and contemporary proverbs share the same structure and function and can be placed side by side in our sermons for dialogue or for dueling. This insight equips preachers to become homiletical sages, comparing and contrasting biblical and contemporary proverbs. This insight provides the motivation for preachers to preach more on proverbial biblical texts, from both the Hebrew scriptures and the New Testament, and to interweave proverbs, both biblical and contemporary, into sermons on other texts as well.

THE SAGE AS AN IMAGE FOR PREACHING MINISTRY

Just as the proverb is a neglected genre in biblical preaching, so the sage is a neglected image for the preaching ministry. The sage is one charged with seeing that the verbal folklore of a given community, specifically proverbs, is nurtured and kept alive from one generation to another. Verbal folklore is the common wisdom possessed by a community, continually re-created in the telling of tales, the citing of proverbs, the singing of ballads, the posing of riddles, and the sharing of superstitions between persons in small-group social interactions.

The Sages of Israel as Models for Preaching Ministry

Throughout Israel's long history, sages coined and taught proverbial wisdom, at diplomatic schools, at court, and in clan and home contexts. Women as well as men were sages, at least in the postexilic period when the Proverbs collection was most likely collected and edited. While a special class of sages may have existed in Israel, many wisdom teachings trace their origins to observation of recurring patterns in human situations and the natural world in the context of family and tribe, farm and town.[13] The aim of these sages was the alignment of human life with these God-given patterns of order toward the goal of personal and community stability and harmony.

Qohelet and Jesus as Models for Our Preaching Ministry

In addition to the sages of Proverbs, Qohelet, the name given to the sage who collected the teachings in Ecclesiastes, and the Synoptic Jesus also influence the contemporary preacher as sage. Both are sages with distinctive outlooks who coin proverbs to confront reigning proverbial wisdom. Qohelet's proverbial sayings subvert traditional wisdom's connection of industry and ethical dealings with good outcomes (Eccl. 9:18). The Synoptic Jesus' proverbial sayings subvert the values of a religious establishment whose goal has become self-preservation (Mark 2:27; Matt. 10:39).

The Preacher as Sage

The preacher as sage keeps the proverbs of the community's common biblical wisdom in circulation among the people. Guided by the presence of Wisdom-in-person, Jesus the crucified and risen sage, the preacher as sage shapes the identity of communities of faith by cultivating an ongoing dialogue between the common wisdom of cultural groups and the biblical wisdom that informs the faith community.[14]

The preacher as sage is alert to cultural proverbs that are in common use in her congregation, both those which are compatible with and those that compete with Christian faith. Her sermons employ both kinds in shaping the community's identity over against surrounding worldviews. The preacher as sage is also alert to proverbs, whether biblical or contemporary, that subvert the practices of both church and culture. Her sermons employ these proverbs to convict church and cultural groups for failure to adhere to the best within their own traditions.

PART ONE
PROVERBS AS WISDOM FOR THE PULPIT

1

Wisdom Is Vindicated by Her Deeds: What Makes Proverbs Work

The proverb belongs to a basic wisdom genre that comes under the heading of the Hebrew term *māšāl*. The term *māšāl* is used in the Hebrew scriptures to refer to a number of literary forms: similitudes, popular sayings, literary aphorisms, taunt songs, bywords, riddles, allegories, and discourses. The term *māšāl* conveys notions of "similitude" and "ruling word." It conveys an authoritative word that makes analogies between items of daily life. The Greek translation of the word *māšāl* is *parabolē*.[1] The parable is a narrative variation on the *māšāl* theme, sharing the proverb's rootedness in daily life and its evocative language.[2]

My definition of proverb corresponds to Roland Murphy's category of "the saying," which he characterizes as a wisdom sentence normally expressed in the indicative mood, based on observation of experience. It is distinguishable from the admonition, which offers a specific command or prohibition.[3]

A proverb is a short saying that expresses a complete thought, which, while most often expressing traditional values, is also capable of subverting them, offering ethical directives in certain new situations that are most often implied rather than directly stated. Maxims and aphorisms are viewed as particular types of proverbs. A maxim is a nonmetaphorical proverb, and an aphorism is a proverb whose author we know and which may well subvert traditional values.[4]

Our focus is on a comparison-contrast between the use of proverbs in Proverbs and two instances of proverb performance beyond that collection. These are the use of proverbial wisdom sayings by Qohelet in Ecclesiastes and by the Jesus of the Synoptic Gospels. My criteria for selecting these examples are twofold: In the first place, they are to a large degree proverbial in form, containing a large proportion of short, isolable nonnarrative forms that look at human life, God, world, and society from a number of different angles. In the second place, Qohelet and the Synoptic Jesus use proverbs to challenge normative wisdom rather than to confirm it, thereby broadening our present understanding of proverbs' homiletical usefulness.[5]

A definition of the proverb that does it justice must take into account its syntactic, semantic, and pragmatic properties. Syntax involves the ways words are combined into clauses and sentences. Semantics involves the relationship between words in combination and the entities to which they refer. Pragmatics refers to the impact of sentences on those who receive them and the influence of context on that reception. In the case of the proverb, as will be discussed in chapter 2, that impact can create or subvert traditional wisdom.

SYNTACTIC PROPERTIES OF THE PROVERB

The syntactic properties of a proverb are as follows: self-containment; fixed form; present or future tense, or equivalent; eschewal of first person; and possession of poetic features. The first four are defining properties of proverbs, while the possession of poetic features is an optional property, found in many but by no means all proverbs.

Proverbs as Self-Contained Linguistic Units

Proverbs are distinguished from proverbial phrases by virtue of the fact that, unlike proverbial phrases ("cool as a cucumber"), they express a complete thought. Proverbs may take the form of a question or a pure predicate: "Can fire be carried in the bosom without burning one's clothes?" (Prov. 6:27). "Forewarned, forearmed."

The Fixed Form of Proverbs

Unlike jokes and folktales, proverbs occur in a fixed form, displaying much the same wording wherever they occur. Fixed does not mean frozen, for proverbs are sturdy enough to undergo changes in wording, being rephrased as questions and even parody without losing their identity as proverbs.

Proverbs as Partial Generalizations

Proverbs are characterized by both specificity and generality. They arise out of specific situations. Their rhetorical intention is to be applied to certain new situations. They themselves, however, operate at a somewhat generalized level of meaning. Proverbs do not depend on hearers or readers' knowing their original context to be understood. So, for example, the Korean proverb "The baby that cries gets the milk" clearly arose out of a specific situation, yet it is sufficiently generalized so that we can apply it to new situations in which, to quote the Western equivalent, squeaky wheels get the grease.[6] Proverbs are partial generalizations, not universal truths for all situations. The proverb's usefulness in new situations is referred to as its "openness to experience," or its *"hermeneutical openness."*

The hermeneutical openness of proverbs is made possible by two syntactic features. Unlike jokes and tales, they most often occur in the present tense. Unlike riddles, aphorisms, and tales, they avoid first-person pronouns and possessives. The present tense gives the proverb a timeless quality, while the absence of the first person gives the proverb a less personalized meaning.[7] The combination of these two elements raises proverbs to a more generalized level of meaning.

Poetic Features in Some Proverbs

The first three syntactic features we have discussed are necessary properties of a proverb. A quality possessed by some but not all proverbs is poetic features such as rhyme, alliteration, parallelism, and repetition. Poetic features help make a statement more memorable, both for speaker and hearer, and increase its chances of becoming a staple unit in the inventory of a language.

SEMANTIC PROPERTIES OF THE PROVERB

The semantic properties of the proverb include topic–comment structures, the frequent presence of metaphor, and hermeneutical openness.

Structural Description of Proverbs

A proverb is "a traditional propositional statement consisting of at least one descriptive element, a descriptive element consisting of a topic and a comment."[8] The topic is the statement's subject, and the comment makes an assertion about the topic concerning its form, function, or action. In the proverb "A good tree cannot bear bad fruit" (Matt. 7:18), the topic is "a good tree" and the comment is "cannot bear bad fruit."

Some proverbs consist of just one descriptive element. For example, "Time flies." More common are multi-descriptive-element proverbs. An example is the Korean proverb, "As for clothes, the newer the better; as for friends, the older the better."[9] Every descriptive element has an image, a message (referent), and an architectural formula. The proverb *image* is the literal level of the proverb. The proverb *message* is the ultimate meaning of the proverb as illustrated by the image. The *architectural formula* is the relationship between the topic and the comment. In a multi-descriptive-element proverb the architectural formula is the relationship between the individual descriptive elements.

The architectural formula is the foundation on which the image rests and the vehicle for the conveyance of the message. Architectural formulas or topic-comment relationships take one of two basic forms: those which contrast and those which compare. Each type of formula has a basic form and variations.[10]

Oppositional proverbs are built along the formula of A does not equal B. "Beggars cannot be choosers." "An estate quickly acquired in the beginning will not be blessed in the end" (Prov. 20:21). Another variation on the oppositional form appears in the "better than" sayings. "Better late than never." "Better is a dinner of vegetables where love is than a fatted ox and hatred with it" (Prov.15:17).

Still another variation of the oppositional form is the "antithetical contradiction," which proverbs share with riddles. "If you have A, then you can't have B." For example, "You can't have your cake and eat it too." Biblical examples include: "You cannot serve God and wealth" (Matt. 6:24). "The wedding guests cannot fast while the bridegroom is with them" (Mark 2:19).

Equational proverbs are built around the basic formula A equals B: "Time is money." "The talk of fools is a rod for their backs" (Prov. 14:3). "The more words, the more vanity" (Eccl. 6:11). A variation of the equational formula is: Where there is A, there is B. "Where there is smoke there is fire." "Where your treasure is, there your heart will be also" (Matt. 6:21). Another equational variation is, A leads to B. "Practice makes perfect." "The plans of the diligent lead surely to abundance, but everyone who is hasty comes only to want" (Prov. 21:5). "The measure you give will be the measure you get back" (Luke 6:38).

The proverb makes connections with new situations by virtue of its topic-comment structure, the logical relationships involved in its architectural formula. When a proverb is cited in a new situation in contemporary life, it becomes a comment on an aspect of the situation that becomes the topic.

Figurative Language in Some Proverbs

The semantic property of metaphor is an important contributor to the proverb's hermeneutical openness. When we employ the term "literal" we refer to those meanings of words that are common to a speaking community, fixed by the norms of usage in that community and inscribed in a lexical code. Classical rhetoric deals with the figurative meanings of words, those meanings that deviate from ordinary use.[11] Traditional rhetorical studies have pointed to several figurative uses of words, including metaphor, metonymy, synecdoche, and simile. The most important one for proverbs is metaphor, in which we speak of one thing in terms suggestive of another. Literal proverbs are often called maxims, while proverbs that picture metaphorical scenes will be referred to as scenic proverbs. Some proverbs lie somewhere between the two extremes of literal and figurative. They include those proverbial sayings that are half literal, half figurative ("Pride feels no pain") and those that can function as literal or nonliteral speech depending on their context. "It never rains but it pours."[12]

Literal and figurative proverbs have the same structure, but they connect with new situations by different means. The literal proverb moves in a vertical way from general to particular, seeking application to particular situations that are a cognitive fit with its generalization (Norrick, 49). ("With the judgment you make you will be judged," Matt. 7:2.) The metaphorical saying begins with a depiction of a specific scene and moves out horizontally seeking metaphorical relationships with the terms of new situations. ("Why do you see the speck in your neighbor's eye, but do not notice the log in your own eye?" Matt. 7:3.) The metaphorical proverb, while expressing a specific, particularized scene, paradoxically can be applied in a wider ranger of situations than a maxim. Its relevance is metaphorically extended by the images it contains as they seek to relate to the components of new situations.

Some proverbs contain metaphor in the interaction between their topic and comment. "The tongue of the righteous is choice silver" (Prov. 10:20). Other proverbs picture a whole scene in vivid, concrete imagery. Israelite sages made metaphorical connections between the realms of nature and human behavior. A door turning on its hinges suggests a lazy person turning over in bed (Prov. 26:14). Clouds that yield no rain suggest people who boast of giving but fail to do so (Prov. 25:14).

Such metaphors are not merely decorative ways of conveying literal meaning. Metaphor's dynamic is "seeing the similarity that has not been seen before in two previously unrelated matrices of thought."[13] The scenes such proverbs depict can be placed by analogy next to the terms of a new situation to spark new insights to guide thought and action. For example, one might apply the proverb "A leopard cannot change its spots" to a relative fighting a substance-abuse problem.

Proverbial metaphor juxtaposes two matrices of thought, the scenic proverb and the terms of the new situation. When the two systems interact, each affects our perception of the other and they produce a new unit of meaning via resemblance (McFague, 37–38). Besides similarity, dissimilarity is crucial to the metaphorical dynamic. For at the literal level the comparison of a leopard's spots and a person's habits is a ridiculous contradiction in terms. One person might view a relative's substance-abuse problem as a leopard's spots, but someone else, objecting to such a pessimistic interpretation, might say, "We are talking about a human being, not a leopard." In making that comment, that person is exposing the subversive nature of metaphor: it operates by dissimilarity between the juxtaposed realms as well as by similarity.

Metaphorical interpretation consists in transforming a contradiction in terms into a meaningful juxtaposition, through the discovery of resemblances between two categories not ordinarily viewed as having anything in common. Metaphorical interpretation is an active resolution of an enigma. In this lies the metaphor's "semantic innovation."[14]

The application of a scenic proverb to a situation represents one interpretation by a particular person, not a binding, universal judgment. Applying a proverb is always somebody's interpretive choice, which is open to the differing views and divergent proverbial choices of others in the community.

Hermeneutical Openness in Proverbs

The essential dynamic of "hermeneutical openness" for both literal and metaphorical proverbs is a dialectic between the general and the specific. If a potentially proverbial saying is too dependent on the specifics of its original situation, it eventually becomes incomprehensible. For example, the English saying "Your father was no glazier" and "Is not the gleaning of the grapes of Ephraim better than the vintage of Abiezer?" (Judg. 8:2). If a proverb is bloated into a blanket truth, it loses its wisdom and can even do great harm. An example of this is the elevation of the proverb "Different strokes for different folks" to the status of universal statement encompassing all choices encountered in American life, from consumer products to moral issues. A biblical example is the explosion of the proverb "If anyone strikes you on the right cheek, turn the other also" (Matt. 5:39) into a universal strategy for all conflictual situations that confront Christians today.

An aphorism, though more closely associated with a particular person than a proverb, shares the proverb's hermeneutical openness. A proverb has been defined as "the wisdom of many, the wit of one."[15] The proverb and the aphorism, the wisdom of many and the wit of one, exist in dialectical relationship: the proverb is an aphorism whose author has been forgotten. An aphorism, if taken to heart by an existing social group, can become a proverb.

2

With the Judgment
You Make:
What Proverbs Do

The proverb has the ability to direct hearers' attitudes and behaviors in specific situations by using indirect language. Unlike
admonitions, which are expressed in the imperative and have a
more limited hermeneutical openness, proverbs are most often
couched in the declarative mode. An example of an admonition is
"Do not judge, so that you may not be judged" (Matt. 7:1). An example of a proverb is "With the judgment you make you will be
judged" (Matt. 7:2). Proverbs report experience, compelling readers
to draw inferences for themselves. Admonitions give commands appealing to the authority of a teacher or parent.[1] So persuasive are
proverbs that often an admonition is substantiated by a proverb (Prov.
1:17; 6:27–29).

PROVERBS THAT CREATE ORDER

The didactic persuasion of proverbs, in most societies historically and
today, has been used to stabilize the status quo, as it was used throughout the centuries of Israel's history. True to form, the proverbs of
Proverbs represent the efforts of both parents and teachers to inculcate in the young norms of respect for community wisdom figures
(sages and parents), moderation in food and drink, abstention from
sexual immorality, respect for the poor, guarding of the tongue, and
industrious habits. Similarly, many contemporary American proverbs
inculcate values that stabilize an individualistic, capitalistic culture.

Proverbs inculcate cultural values in two broad ways: they serve as vehicles for education and as an attempt to resolve ambiguity in social interactions. Because they are both brief and memorable, proverbs are well qualified, whether in oral or literate cultures, to help a society retain and transmit a traditional body of ethical guidelines for conduct.

Proverbs are directed at "cultural ambiguity." When a situation arises that threatens to disrupt the smooth working of life, proverbs, impersonally phrased and appealing to precedent, offer direction among alternative paths. They offer a basis for either praising or censuring another's choices in ambiguous situations.[2] For example, Proverbs depicts "the two ways," the way of wisdom and the way of folly, and the two types of people who pursue the paths, one to life, the other to death.

Because they are impersonal and indirect, proverbs can minimize interpersonal friction.[3] To a consistently negative parishioner a pastor could get away with saying, "It is easier to tear down than to build up" more easily than, "Why do you always have to be so negative?" Proverbs, as declarative statements about experience, not direct addresses or commands, enjoy maximum authority with minimal offense. Hence their popularity with diplomats!

The proverb is capable of subverting the status quo as well as serving it. Both functions are possible because of the proverb's key cultural function, one it shares with folklore in general. It expresses the basic premises or "cultural axioms" that underlie the thought and action of a given group of people. When proverbs express the worldview of those in power, they inculcate the dominant status quo. When they express a worldview of a group on the underside of power relationships, proverbs subvert the status quo. For example, "Black is beautiful" and "The blacker the berry the sweeter the juice" subvert a host of the dominant culture's prejudicial proverbs. Other contemporary examples of this subversive dynamic come from the women's movement's challenge to traditional views of women. A proverb expressing the traditional conviction of women's total dependency on men is "A woman without a man is like a fish without water." This traditional assumption is challenged by the proverb "A woman without a man is like a fish without a bicycle."

In his study of the social function of moral exhortation in the ancient Near East, Leo Perdue discerns two types of social groups that

employ moral exhortation, including proverbs, for two widely different purposes: the social paradigm of order and that of conflict. The
paradigm of order projects a world order as originating at creation and
continuing to categorize and regulate existing elements into a harmonious whole.[4] The primary social function of moral instruction,
including proverbs, in this paradigm is the legitimatization of traditional norms. Proverbs are used to preserve or stabilize the existing
social order by means of an appeal to duty, self-interest, and obedience. Immoral behavior produces chaos in every sphere and is viewed
as a threat to communal and individual life (Purdue, 8).

In keeping with the conservative nature of the order paradigm,
Proverbs recommend obedience to community wisdom figures as a
means of motivating the young to avoid the threat posed by foolish
behavior that foments social chaos. Proverbs stressing behavior that
leads to orderly, stable, harmonious extended family life predominate
in the book of Proverbs.[5]

The theological and social function of the Proverbs collection is,
as James Williams characterizes it, a "wisdom of order," as contrasted
with Jesus' and Qohelet's "wisdom of counter-order." The stability-
seeking impulse of the wisdom of order reveals itself in motifs such as
the consistency of retribution, the importance of wise utterance and
self-control of the individual, and submission to the authority of the
Fathers.[6]

The downside of teachings that reflect this wisdom of order is that
they can tend toward the ideological control of less powerful groups,
among them women, children, and the poor. For example, an ancient
Korean proverb says, "Three men determine the fate of every
woman" (her father, her husband, and her son). This Confucian tradition has been the ironclad rule in Korean society for centuries, serving as a sanction for women's subordination and abuse. It is beginning
to be challenged by Korea's recently formed Women Church and by
the greater latitude for women's contributions in American immi-
grant churches.[7] Clearly, moral exhortation can become a powerful
means of ideological control in the process of social formation. For
this reason misogynist proverbs (Prov. 9:13; 11:22; 12:4; 19:13;
21:19), proverbs that commend corporal punishment of children
(Prov. 13:24; 23:13, 14), and those which attribute poverty to laziness (Prov. 24:30–34) need to be subverted in our preaching.
Proverbs that commend caution in the face of political power (20:2)

need to be subverted by those which point to the need for rulers' submission to God. (Prov. 16:9f.; 20:26; 21:1; 25:5).

A chilling example of the ideological use of proverbs is the National Socialists' use of proverbs and other forms of folklore to lionize German racial purity and to discredit the Jewish population during the 1930s and 1940s. Hitler's advisers recognized the persuasive power of the proverbial form and both coined and culled proverbs from biblical and folk sources, reinterpreting them to convey the message of racial purity and destruction of the Jews.

A favorite proverb of the National Socialists was an older German proverb, "The common good takes precedence over self-interest," which they interpreted to mean that everyone had better work together to build the war machinery as a defense of the fatherland against outside aggression.[8] Scholars of Nazi proverbs published collections of sayings to inculcate the virtues of mental and physical health, love of country, and, above all, the fight against alien elements. "There is no better dowry than a healthy body and mind." "Single, sinful." "Three things make the best couples: same blood, same passion, and same age." Proverbs for the raising of young children, defined as "training for subordination," include "He who commands well, is well obeyed"; "Obedience is the foundation of all order" (Mieder, 239–42).

The moral instruction of the order model tends to legitimate the power and position held by the normally male aristocracy.[9] Language and the norms for its use are controlled by the dominant group. Marginal groups have limited means for expressing their experience and worldview, and eventually tend to fall silent. The proverb works against this silencing process by virtue of several of its qualities: it is ubiquitous, adaptable, brief, arises out of everyday experience, and is accessible to all groups in a society regardless of educational attainments or technological skills.

PROVERBS THAT SUBVERT ORDER

Groups on the underside of asymmetrical power relationships often operate within a social paradigm of conflict that employs the proverbial genre used by dominant groups but gives it a new content. An example would be Qohelet's satirizing of the "better than" proverbial form in Ecclesiastes 7:1–2: "A good name is better than precious ointment, and the day of death, than the day of birth. It is better to go to the house of mourning than to go to the house of feasting." An example from the Synoptic sayings attributed to Jesus is: "The sabbath was made for humankind, and not humankind for the sabbath" (Mark 2:27), which expresses Jesus' subversion of the superficial ritualism of his day.

In the context of the controversy and crisis contemporary to each, Qohelet and the Synoptic Jesus use the traditional proverbial wisdom form, both quoting and coining proverbs. They employ it, in part in continuity with the worldview of normative wisdom, but more characteristically to challenge those prevailing wisdom teachings. Qohelet and Jesus use the aphoristic wisdom of counter-order to offer an intra-wisdom critique of the wisdom tradition using its own forms, thereby empowering those forms to express a new voice in a new age. They redefine the situation of their hearers into a worldview that challenges the normative tradition of their day.

In their use of the normative tradition's oral forms to challenge the dominant worldview, Qohelet and the Synoptic Jesus reveal themselves to be *subversive sages*. The term, rather than being viewed as a contradiction in terms, becomes a helpful framework within which to understand the activity of preaching on proverbs. It clarifies the role of the preacher as one who consults scripture to at times confirm, but at other times to challenge conventional cultural insights. A subversive sage is one who is alert to the ways contemporary subversive proverbs challenge the worldviews that dominate culture and aspects of the church's life as well.

The capacity of proverbs to both mirror and challenge cultural worldviews from generation to generation accounts for their enduring popularity as a form of cultural rhetoric. Some recent folklore studies suggest that the repertoire of proverbs of the average American is shrinking. It is more accurate to say that it is changing, with some old favorites dropping out and others, which better reflect the language, politics, and technology of contemporary life, taking their place. While proverbs are still used to instruct persons in traditional values, increasingly they are also being used in an innovative way, that is, they are changed and twisted until they fit the demands of our contemporary age.[10] One example of innovation is the "proverb parody." A parody is an imitation of the style of a work treating a serious subject in a humorous or ridiculing manner. Though often humorous, proverb parodies offer a formidable challenge to traditional values of honest, frugal, moderate living.

Some contemporary examples are: "Chaste makes waste." "God help those who get caught helping themselves." "The best things in life are for a fee." "You can't tell a book by its movie." "No nukes is good nukes." "Crime pays—be a lawyer." "All that glitters can be yours." "Speak softly and wear a loud shirt."[11]

Jesus and Qohelet coin aphorisms that subvert complacent, superficial attitudes and behaviors that do not do justice to the complexity of life and the sovereignty of God over human affairs. Qohelet's aphorisms undercut the traditional tendency to guarantee order as the outcome of wisdom. For example, "In much wisdom is much vexation, and those who increase knowledge increase sorrow" (Eccl. 1:18). Jesus' aphorisms sketch a subversive way of life more in keeping with God's already- and not-yet-present kingdom. For example, "Whoever wishes to be great among you must be your servant, and whoever wishes to be first among you must be your slave" (Matt. 20:26, 27).

A contemporary example of proverbs' subversive dynamic is the parody of "Life is short; play hard": "Life is short; pray hard." "Seeing is believing" is subverted by "Believing is seeing."

The subversive use of proverbs is made possible by two of their syntactic and semantic properties discussed in chapter 1: their quality as partial rather than universal generalizations and their frequent use of metaphor. As a limited generalization, any given proverb may or may not be appropriate in a particular situation; its truth is conditional and relative, not absolute. Proverbs originate as the fresh insights of individual sages as they observe and evaluate daily life around them, and are intended to be placed back into daily situations guided by the wisdom of their contemporary users. Proverbs were never meant to be taken as unambiguous, universal statements of "that which really is."[12]

The fact that they sound like general truths, due to their impersonal, generalized syntax, and that they appear in collections, often without contextual clues, can make us forget that they are actually partial generalizations, appropriate for some situations and not for others, a fact driven home by the existence of diametrically opposed proverbs: "Absence makes the heart grow fonder"; "Out of sight, out of mind."

The Israelite sages included in their collection proverbs recommending varying responses to how to answer a fool, how to view wealth, and how to view the poor, because they recognized proverbs' nature as partial generalizations, which require wisdom to be employed wisely. Proverbs do not express or speak to all of human experience. The worldviews of suppressed groups, whose life situations are not represented by normative proverbs, become the seedbeds of subversive wisdom.

This subversion was an integral part of the wisdom process of the Israelite sages represented in Proverbs. Their proverbial wisdom was not a rigid core of beliefs that ostracized alternative views, but rather a grasp of reality's complexity and an openness to varying interpretations. Elizabeth Faith Huwiler, in her contextual study of Proverbs' sentence wisdom, insists that discussion, modification, and even subversion of prevailing tenets were an integral part of this ongoing wisdom process.[13]

A second property that equips proverbs to subvert order is their frequent use of metaphor. Peter Seitel calls proverbs' cultural function the "social use of metaphor."[14] When a contemporary proverb user cites a scenic proverb in relation to a particular situation, drawing a parallel, say, between someone searching for meaning in a materialistic culture and someone searching for figs in a thornbush, she is establishing a metaphorical link between aspects of the proverb and the contemporary situation. Such comparisons suggest new ways of looking at a situation, but do not constitute the only way of looking at it. This opens the door for proverbs to subvert other proverbs, for suppressed groups to devise proverbs that subvert those of dominant groups, and for suppressed groups to keep a self-critical edge in their own proverb use.

The quality of proverbs as partial generalizations rather than universal truths and their frequent use of metaphor are what John J. Collins calls the "seeds of a debunking tendency" akin to that of prophecy and parable.[15] Proverbs, both literal and metaphorical, can expose and challenge our underlying cultural axioms and point toward alternatives. This subverts the traditional assumption that biblical proverbs' job description is limited to preserving order, leaving subversion in the hands of prophecy and parables.

3

No Good Tree Bears Bad Fruit: How to Create Sermons on Proverbs

Proverbs need to interact with a reader if their meaning is to be activated. The same is true of imaginative literature. Novels, like proverbs, are a form of pragmatic literary communication which functions to reveal something new about the social, historical context called reality that could come about in no other way. The interaction between text and reader is the focus of a method of literary interpretation known as reader-response theory. A key theorist in this field is Wolfgang Iser. His depiction of the way text and reader interact in the production of meaning, as set forth in his book *The Act of Reading,* helps us map the interaction between proverb and reader for preaching sermons on proverbs.

THE INTERACTION BETWEEN PROVERB AND READER

While Iser developed his theories in relation to the genre of novels, they are applicable to the much shorter proverb as well. Whether a novel or a proverb, both text and reader contribute to the production of meaning that results from what Iser calls "the act of reading." The interaction between these two poles forms the ground plan for Iser's theory of literary communication.

What the Text Does

Proverbs and novels share basic components which Iser calls *perspectives.* Novels have an author, characters, plot, and space marked out for the reader.[1] Proverbs have as their author collective wisdom, or in the case of aphorisms, an innovative individual. Their topic and comment are analogous to the novel's characters, the relationship between them forms a sort of plot, and the space marked out for the reader is the proverb's hermeneutical openness.

Both proverb and novel have a *repertoire,* which is that combination of historical-social and literary conventions or norms that an author chooses from his social context to combine in the literary work. Iser believes that profound literature is generated by an author's sense that certain viewpoints are not being represented in dominant culture. He calls this gnawing sense that something is lacking *negativity* (Iser, 227). An example of this sense of lack at work is: "For those who want to save their life will lose it, and those who lose their life for my sake, and for the sake of the gospel, will save it" (Mark 8:35). This aphorism originated in Jesus' sense of the inadequacy of traditional wisdom's theological norm that wisdom leads to gain and long life, whereas folly leads to loss and death.

This sense of something lacking or distorted in our habitual outlooks describes a fundamental dynamic, not only of the creation, but also of the reception of literary works. The reader, in responding to the norms the author has chosen and combined in a work, gets a sense of those viewpoints which are not represented in normative wisdom and begins to reevaluate his habitual assumptions in light of this lack (225f.). The effect of this process on the reader is what Iser means by defamiliarization. For a moment, the reader observes her world from the outside looking in, and, recognizing the deficiencies of traditional norms, questions the given world (225f.).

Some literature supports prevailing systems. The repertoire of didactic and propagandist literature takes over intact the thought system already familiar to its readers, seeking to train readers in prevailing social codes against threats to its validity (77ff.). When a work seeks to bolster the weakness of a system, as was the case in the postexilic proverbs collection, a text will strive for a high degree of conformity between its repertoire and that of its perceived readers. If the weak points of a system of thought are to be exposed, as in the case of Qohelet and the Synoptic Jesus, the balance will shift toward disparity and reassessment. In either case, a reader may or may not allow the text to realize its goal. The reader may instead subvert the text, seeking to defamiliarize the text to its own norms.

There is a second dynamic that fuels communication between text and reader in addition to the sense of lack. It is *indeterminacy,* the sense of the unknown (the blank). "The blank designates a vacancy in the overall system of the text, the filling of which brings about an interaction of textual patterns" (182). With proverbs, the blank between reader and proverbs is caused by the fact that the specific situation out of which a proverb arose is unknown to the reader. The reader fills the blank by applying the proverb to new situations (182ff.).

The Strategies

The strategies are the structure by which the norms of the repertoire are organized. They function to make the repertoire accessible to the reader.

Strategy #1: Foreground-Background

This strategy is the link between the norms selected for the text's repertoire and the dominant thought systems that surround the literary work. The elements the author has chosen for inclusion become the foreground and their surrounding context becomes the background (92ff.).

Strategy #2: Theme-Horizon

Theme-horizon is the strategy that describes the internal workings of the text. The norms of the repertoire are expressed in the text through the narrator, characters, plot, and space marked out for the reader (96ff.). The theme is like the "You are here" arrow on a map. The horizon is like the rest of the map. The act of reading is a temporal process in which the reader can dwell in only one perspective at a time (the theme), but in which her experience of the perspectives that have preceded this moment of reading form the horizon of memory and anticipation which influence this moment.

What the Reader Does

The textual structures of repertoire and strategies invite the reader's twofold responses: the wandering viewpoint and consistency building.

The Wandering Viewpoint

The wandering viewpoint describes the reader's processing presence in the text. A literary work is composed of a succession of sentences, each of which depends on what came before it to be comprehended and aims at that which comes after it. The reader's presence in the text is at the intersection of remembrance of what has gone before and anticipation of what lies ahead. The reading process is a continual interplay between memories and expectations, which are modified as the reader interacts with each succeeding sentence. In a novel, the wandering viewpoint constantly switches between the textual perspectives of narrator, author, plot, characters, and space left open for the reader, in a process called "reciprocal spotlighting" (114).

This image of the spotlight is an apt analogy for a proverb, with its compression of the observation of life-narratives into brief evaluative statements. Like the binoculars one finds at scenic overlooks, the proverb beckons us to pull over just for a moment and look through it out over the landscape of our journey, looking for situations to which it can bring ethical clarity. The proverb represents one stop on the wandering viewpoint's journey, one still-life moment between remembrance and anticipation.

Consistency Building

The wandering viewpoint is not a mere meandering through a random and fragmented time flow. Its goal is the building of a consistent interpretation as the reader moves through the interacting textual perspectives. The perspectives exist in potential correlation with one another so that several readers' differing interpretations, while not identical, can be at least mutually comprehensible, because they result from connections of standing structures in the text. The reader makes selections in favor of specific connections among perspectives in each sequential moment of reading. With a proverb, the correlation is the potential analogies between the proverb and contemporary situations made possible by the proverb's syntactic, semantic properties. While not all interpreters would agree with the application of a given proverb to a given situation, it remains a comprehensible connection.

Consistent interpretations are formed when one possibility is selected and the rest excluded. Readers make selections in favor of that which is familiar to them on the basis of past experiences (125–26). Excluded possibilities remain on the outskirts of the reader's attention, distracting him from a sense of participation in the text into a posture of partial detachment and questioning of the validity of the consistent interpretation he has just formed. In the case of a proverb, the excluded possibilities are those situations which the proverb does not fit which call for other, perhaps opposing proverbs. An example is Qohelet's sense that the pursuit of wisdom leads, not to the discernment of orderly patterns in life, but to an awareness of life's inequities and tragedies. "In much wisdom is much vexation, and those who increase knowledge increase sorrow" (Eccl. 1:18).

FROM PROVERB TO SERMON

Norms of the Proverb

Looking at proverbs through the lens of a text's repertoire generates insight into the social, historical context of sayings in collections: Proverbs, Ecclesiastes, and the Synoptic sayings.

Historical-Social Norms

Through a study of proverbs' historical, social, and literary norms there comes a clearer view of how proverbs reflect the influence of their collective context and their potential, taken individually, to speak from it, offering commentary on aspects of our contemporary context. The two functional identities of proverbs—proverbs in texts and proverbs as discrete texts—are both given credit.

The preacher needs to ask a series of questions, the first being, What is the most likely historical-social context in which this proverb was collected? Is it a social model primarily of order or of conflict? In that context, is the proverb being used primarily to inculcate existing wisdom (familiarize the reader with it and defamiliarize the reader to threats to it)? Or is it being used primarily to subvert aspects of existing normative wisdom (defamiliarize the reader to it)? Is this a proverb that creates order, or one that subverts order? If it is a Synoptic proverb, is Jesus portrayed as using a proverb in continuity with existing wisdom, or, in a conflict situation, using a proverb (or coining an aphorism) to subvert existing normative wisdom?

Theological Norms

What theological norms of the wisdom literature are encapsulated in this proverb? This question views proverbs, not as isolated texts, but as texts within texts. Proverbs need to be viewed in the theological context that shapes the literary work within which they find themselves. An evangelist's distinctive theological portrayal of Jesus needs to be taken into account in preaching on proverbs that appear in that Gospel. One of the key theological norms of Proverbs is that human life is lived in the context of an inscrutable, sovereign God. This mitigates the potential hubris of those proverbs which claim that certain human behaviors can all but guarantee certain outcomes.

A proverb must also be set within its broader canonical context. When preaching on proverbs from the Hebrew Scriptures, this means that preaching on proverbs of order must take into account the existence of proverbs of subversion, which challenge human constructs. Preaching on subversive proverbs must take into account the existence of proverbs that inculcate a legitimate measure of personal and social stability based on God's gift of recurring patterns in the realms of human and natural life.

Wisdom literature depicts God as guiding the community in a lifelong search for patterns of order that begins and ends as God's gift. Preaching on proverbial wisdom texts in the context of the biblical canon means acknowledging the existence of other genres with their distinctive depictions of divine activity: direct addresses to the prophets, mighty saving acts, and promises of imminent apocalyptic judgment and vindication.

Considering canonical context in preaching proverbs of the Synoptic Jesus means preaching on proverbs in the context of the cross-resurrection kerygma of the Christian faith. In this context, the subversive sayings attributed to Jesus the Sage, which defamiliarize us to habitual attitudes and behaviors, become homiletical vehicles through which the risen Christ, present to us through the Holy Spirit, can guide us in the kinds of subversion that once led to the Sage's death and now embody his ongoing counter-order presence in our midst. Preaching on Jesus' proverbs in the canonical context of his death and resurrection is an affirmation of his identity as Wisdom-in-person then and now. It means that our proverbial preaching offers hearers not only guidance in against-the-grain living, but empowerment for that living that human observation and encouragement alone could never mediate.

Literary Norms

How is this proverb set in its surrounding literary context? Is the proverb presented as addressing a particular situation, or is it part of a proverbial cluster on a particular subject, such as the sayings on wise and foolish speech that abound in chapter 10 of Proverbs or the cluster of sayings regarding blessings and woes in Luke 6:20–26? With regard to Synoptic sayings, is Jesus depicted as using the proverb or aphorism in response to a particular challenge to his and his disciples' practices? (Matt. 19:24; Mark 2:19; 2:27; 9:35).[2]

Are there literary connections between the proverb and the text that precedes and follows it? Is it positioned to provide warrant for an admonition that either precedes or follows it? (Prov. 6:27, 28; 19:20, 21). Is it positioned to subvert or relativize the truth of an adjacent saying? (Prov. 18:10–12). Jesus is frequently depicted as using proverbs or aphorisms to subvert, and outright oppose, existing proverbs and practices (Matt. 5:38, 39; Mark 7:15; Luke 4:23, 24).

Perspectives of the Proverb

Who is the narrator? Is it anonymous common wisdom? Is it that of a particular person, as in the case of the aphorisms of Qohelet or Jesus?

What is the topic and comment? If it is a scenic metaphorical proverb, what images does it employ? What scene does it picture?

What is the relationship between the topic and comment? Are they being equated or contrasted? Does the proverb, whether literal or figurative, suggest connections with contemporary situations facing the life of the preacher's congregation?

What attitudes and norms of conduct are subverted? For example, the proverb "Those who trust in their riches will wither, but the righteous will flourish like green leaves" (Prov. 11:28) flies in the face of materialism as the foundation of a life represented by the contemporary proverb "Money makes the world go round." It is itself negated by the evidence all around us of the rich flourishing and the righteous withering. What are the limits of the proverb's wisdom as a partial truth? Are there situations in life with which the proverb is not an apt fit and in which it could even do more harm than good? Whether preaching on an order proverb or an order-subverting proverb, the preacher reflects on what situations negate the proverb, exposing the limits of its truth. Does this proverb have an opposite that directly expresses those limits?

The Proverb as Scenic Overlook

In a narrative the reader's action in moving through the narrative may be described as the formation of consistent interpretations (consistency building). Applied to the proverb, the reader's action becomes a gathering of a constellation of experiences to the proverb, with which the reader deems it to be an apt fit. The reader uses the proverb as a scenic overlook, highlighting situations that need its wisdom in his life and world. Gathering a constellation of experiences to the proverb is the basic dynamic of the reading and the preaching of a proverb, as can be seen in the sermons in chapters 8 and 9.

The sermon hearer is offered the proverb as a wisdom tool both to evaluate the past and to guide the future. This offering of the proverb's wisdom by a homiletical sage is always a community process as well. In the context of corporate worship, preaching proverbs clarifies the faith community's collective wisdom for its ongoing life in, over against, and for the world.

PART TWO

PROVERBS THAT CREATE AND SUBVERT ORDER

4

The Wise,
When Rebuked, Will Love You:
Biblical Proverbs That
Create Order

This chapter focuses on the historical-social, literary, and theological norms of biblical proverbs of order found in the book of Proverbs. Proverbs is comprised of four major collections of wisdom instructions and sayings, to which several smaller collections of sayings, instructions, numerical progressions, and an acrostic have been appended.[1] Chapters 1—9 are a collection of sayings, instructions, didactic narratives, and poetic passages, whose title, "the proverbs of Solomon," also serves as title to the entire book of thirty-one chapters. They reflect on the paradoxical nature of wisdom as both a divine gift and a human search, and they command hearers to choose wisdom and the benefits she brings to those who embark on her path. These chapters introduce a personification of Wisdom as one who had an active role in creation (3:19–20; 8:22f.) and who now stands amid daily life calling those who pass by to choose her path rather than the path of folly and death (1:20f.; 8:1f.).

Proverbs contains three other major collections. Two of these collections are ascribed to Solomon (10:1–22:16; 25:1–29:27), reflecting the tendency to associate proverbial material with Solomon. A third group of sayings currently has no ascription, but their title in the Septuagint was "the words of the wise" (22:17–24:22). They show remarkable similarities to *The Instruction of Amenemope*, a collection of Egyptian teachings which originated in scribal circles. The didactic tone of these sayings emphasizes the virtues of silence and composure. Chapters 10—15 are characterized by antithetical parallelism, while 16:1–22:16 are characterized primarily by synonymous parallelism. Both types of proverb structures serve to distinguish sharply between wise and foolish behavior and people, and to elaborate the evils of folly and the benefits of wisdom, particularly those of wise speech. The collection in chapters 25—29 is introduced as the proverbs of Solomon transmitted by the men of Hezekiah (king of Judah in the time of Isaiah at the end of the eighth century). Chapters 25—27 contain many striking comparisons and metaphors and relatively little antithetical parallelism. In chapters 28—29, these features are reversed, and the just-unjust antithesis is more frequent.[2]

Chapter 31 is a poem on the excellent woman (*'ēšet ḥayil*), organized as an acrostic poem which serves as a summary for the whole book. It uses the female manager of a household as a metaphor for envisioning Woman Wisdom, lauding her for the same reasons Woman Wisdom has been praised in the preceding thirty chapters: she illuminates and protects her household.[3]

Using the definition of proverbial properties (set forth in chapter 1), the following sayings qualify as proverbs.

> In chapters 1—9: 1:7; 1:17; 1:32; 3:32; 6:27, 28; 9:7, 8, 9, 10
> The entirety of "the proverbs of Solomon" collection: chapters 10:1–22:29
> In the collection entitled "Sayings of the Wise": 24:5; 24:6
> In the collection entitled "these also (belong) to the wise": 24:27
> The entirety of "the proverbs of Solomon (the work of the men of Hezekiah)": 25:1–29:27. (Exceptions: 25:2–10, 12–17, 21, 22)

The proverbs of the collection come from a variety of settings in the life of the Israelite community: clan, court, home, and wisdom school. Most contemporary scholars agree that, while the collection no doubt contains many preexilic sayings, the book of Proverbs was collected and edited during the postexilic period.[4]

THE NORMS OF PROVERBS

Historical-Social Norms

It is likely that Proverbs was put in its final form in Judah during the time after the rise of Cyrus but before that of Alexander. The Babylonian conquest destroyed most of the southern kingdom of Judah and resulted in the deportation of the major landholders, the king, court, Jerusalem nobility, and upper classes of surrounding settlements. Exiles who returned under Persian sponsorship reasserted their right to the land against the peasants who now occupied it.[5]

During the period of the monarchy, the primary purveyors of wisdom had been members of the professional scribal class connected with the Judean royal administration. With the shift to the postexilic period came a shift in the educational context of wisdom activity from preexilic court to postexilic extended family. Proverbs presupposes a community whose profile coincides with the leading members of the postexilic extended families: educated descendants of the Judean elite who were deported to Babylon, who possessed an ancient literary and didactic heritage but did not apply it toward any professional end. These lay heads of paternal estates, along with the priestly leadership of the restored Temple, wielded social power in the postexilic community. Despite their urban sophistication they were engaged in agriculture and combined practical farming advice with elegant poetic figures from the world of agriculture. These postexilic sages were concerned with the education of a broader laity, not with the education of a scribal professional class, though traces of that earlier goal survive in 22:17–29 (Washington, 166f.).

The emphasis in Proverbs on the mother as well as the father as the source of wisdom also points to a postexilic social setting, for in that period, the inculcation of family values became crucial to reestablishing a basis for a workable social organization. This final level of redaction is evident in 1:6; 6:20; 23:22–25; and 31:10–31. The association of wisdom with the mother suggests the postexilic social situation, when the monarchy and its institutions had collapsed and family values and education at home became more important.[6]

Historical-social conditions unique to the early postexilic period allowed for a female-personified figure to become a religious metaphor. With power decentralized from court and Temple to home, with traditional male mediating figures of king and priest toppled, a new kind of mediator was needed. The king was the symbolic locus of God's blessing, the mediator of God's revelation to the covenant people (Camp, 282). Wisdom drew to herself these traditional roles, which had been lost, and at the same time the newly validated roles of women in home and community.

Woman Wisdom as a metaphor in Proverbs draws to herself the qualities associated with "the feminine" in Israelite culture: an involvement in the mundane specifics of daily experience that women and wisdom share. Though often excluded from formal, public arenas of political and legal decision making, women occupy a role as informal historians and social critics and arbiters of morality. Given the place of women in the traditional social order, it makes sense that wisdom, a highly pragmatic religious tradition, would be imaged in female form.

The connection between women and daily experience finds expression in six biblical motifs that inform Woman Wisdom: the wife as household manager and as counselor to her husband; the lover; the harlot and adulteress; the wise woman; the use by women of indirect means to achieve divine ends; and the activity of women as authenticators of tradition.

These last two motifs contribute to the pairing of Woman Wisdom with a body of proverbs. Female characters in biblical narratives, forced behind the scenes in a society that accords them little legitimate authority, use indirect but effective means of persuasion. Examples are Rebekah (Gen. 27), Tamar (Gen. 38), Shiphrah and Puah (Exodus 1), Moses' mother and sister (Exodus 2), Ruth and Naomi, Michal (1 Sam. 19:11–17), the wise woman of Tekoa (2 Samuel 14), and Esther. Given the fact that indirection is the rhetorical tactic of the proverb, this pattern would contribute to Wisdom's being personified as female (124).

Wisdom, paired with several collections of sayings, becomes their speaker and authenticator. This is in keeping with the tradition of validating written traditions by connecting them with a single, divinely gifted individual. Examples are the pairing of David and the Psalms, Moses and the Pentateuch, the prophets and the prophetic books, Huldah the prophetess in relation to Deuteronomy, and Esther in relation to the practices of Purim. So Woman Wisdom, in response to the loss of the kingly mediator of God's revelation to the people, authenticates a body of authoritative writings that were accepted as the divinely willed means of revelation (140f.).

The probable social context for the final redaction of Proverbs has been explored. The question now arises: What historical-social norms have been chosen from this milieu for inclusion in the repertoire of this proverbs collection? The overarching historical-social norm that characterizes the proverbs of the book of Proverbs is the norm of order.

Wisdom Leads to Life

Proverbs' meta-norm of order, the centerpiece of their historical-social repertoire, is expressed in the association of wisdom with the image of life. Life is both the goal and the substance of the wise person's search for order and knowledge. Wisdom herself is a tree of life to those who lay hold of her (3:18). Life is characterized by two words *(ḥayyîm* and *nepeš)*. *Ḥayyîm* is defined quantitatively as long years and qualitatively as prosperity and honor, the benefits that accrue to the one who chooses wisdom.[7]

Life is also described as *nepeš,* the living, inward being whose life resides in breath and blood. When one chooses wisdom, one is promised that this inward life will manifest itself in *ḥayyîm,* long years and all that goes with it. One is also promised that Wisdom will guard *nepeš* from harm.[8]

At the communal level, life manifests itself in the establishment of a community characterized by social stability. The pursuit of personal and social stability expressed in terms of *šālôm* (peace, harmony, welfare) is the vocation of the sage. "Her [Wisdom's] ways are ways of pleasantness and all her paths are *šālôm*" (Prov. 3:17).[9] The sage recognizes that placing one's life under the tutelage of God's gift of wisdom positions one on the way to *šālôm,* for such obedience gives length of days and years of life and abundant welfare (*šālôm,* Prov. 3:1–2).

Act Leads to Consequence

Israel's sages noticed that certain patterns of behavior lead to certain patterns of consequences. Obedience to authority, industry, and control of tongue, passions, and appetites has an intrinsic connection with health, long life, good reputation, and a degree of prosperity. Opposite choices lead to negative outcomes, chaos, and ultimately death. Wisdom as consisting in concrete daily choices is conveyed by two images: wisdom as the art of steering, and wisdom as the choice of one road in life over another. Interestingly, these two images also make frequent appearances in Egyptian instruction literature. Wisdom in

Proverbs is described as the "art of steering" (*taḥbūlôt*, which means strategy or steering; 1:5) through the ambiguous passages of life toward the goal of *šālôm*. Such steering skill is compared to warriors who realize that planning and skill are essential to victory (Prov. 24:5–6). The term *taḥbūlôt* probably originated in the nautical image of "steering" or "guiding" a boat by pulling ropes or cords.[10]

The image of the path or way of life expresses this journey of steering toward a destination by means of choices of conduct. The first nine chapters of Proverbs refer to the two ways: the way of life and the way of death. Two groups of people travel these two ways: the wise and the foolish. The wise person, utilizing proverbs as an ethical resource, steers along paths of behavior that lead to personal and social order, *šālôm*. Fools, those who are wise in their own eyes, disdain instruction, rely on their own ingenuity, and become hopelessly lost along winding footpaths.[11]

The Israelite wisdom tradition represented by Proverbs, like Egyptian wisdom instruction, was a wisdom of order. As such it contained dynamics that tended toward rigid ideology as well as subversive elements that worked against such rigidity. Israelite wisdom does not subordinate Yahweh to a causal principle of order. Rather, it seeks that order out of its acknowledgment of Yahweh's sovereignty over the human and the natural realms.

The act-consequence connection was made more tenuous by the acknowledgment that human wisdom is limited, that God is inscrutable, and that, therefore, human existence contains a degree of unpredictability that cannot be reduced to a formula. The "limit proverbs" (16:1, 2, 9; 19:21; 20:24; 21:30–31), based on observation of situations in which the best-laid plans founder, repeatedly remind the community of these insights. The fear of the Lord is the motivation for following wisdom; resultant good effects are a secondary consideration. The motive for aligning human conduct with wisdom is to serve the purposes of the Creator (16:1, 9; 21:1).[12]

Israelite wisdom works against an absolutizing of one viewpoint by allowing contradictory proverbs to coexist in the collection (Prov. 26:4, 5) and by including clusters of proverbs that represent differing outlooks on certain life themes, such as wealth and poverty, speech and silence.

Speech and silence is a prime example of a topic on which the sages acknowledged that various situations called for various responses. The sages had great respect for the potency of speech as vehicle of healing and life or of destruction.[13] Chapter 10 is an extended proverb cluster dealing with wise and foolish speech, and this theme is prominent in chapters 10—15 and chapters 17 and 18, as well as chapter 25:11–20. A number of proverbs counsel silence or gentleness in speech as a wise course of action (15:1). Silence, however, can also be a sign of stupidity (17:28). At times harsh speech and rebuke are called for (10:10; 25:12; 28:23). Identification with the wisdom group and its motivations and goals helped to ensure that one's choices of strategies with regard to speech—gentle, harsh, or none at all—would be life-giving rather than death-dealing in various situations.[14]

The Proverbs collection contains proverbs that represent several views of wealth and poverty, the result of combining traditions of originally disparate origins. One outlook on poverty, most likely originating in Judean village life, is the fatalistic acceptance of poverty as a brutal reality of life. These proverbs reflect the point of view of those who are themselves poor, an outlook that appears frequently in Proverbs 10—22.[15] Still another view is that poverty is the deserved result of drunkenness and laziness, a perspective that reflects the viewpoint of those who have not known poverty.[16]

A third perspective discourages mistreatment of the poor as inappropriate to the truly wise person (17:5). This perspective is shaped by the depiction of Yahweh in the legal codes, prophetic literature, and psalms as the protector of the weak par excellence.[17] The protection of the poor is also emphasized in the proverbs that come from the Amenemope collection (22:22–23; 23:10–11) despite its origins in scribal elitist circles. They condemn unjust gain and reveal reservations about the value of wealth (23:4–5). Absent from these sayings is the doctrine that prosperity is a reward for righteousness.[18]

In Proverbs, viewed in its entirety, sayings that blame the poor for their poverty are qualified by those which place relative stress on concern for the poor. This concern, however, remains within the realm of a charity that does not profoundly subvert the status quo. The sages who edited Proverbs, as well as Job and Qohelet, were most likely not the direct victims of poverty. The basic ethos of proverbial wisdom in Proverbs is that the social status quo is worth preserving without serious change.[19] Even the subversive sage Qohelet is a traditionalist on the subject of wealth and poverty, viewing poverty as grounds for skeptical despair rather than social criticism. Jesus goes farther than his predecessors in his criticism of existing social practices and in his subversive teachings on the role of the poor in the reign of God.

Differing interpretations of wealth and poverty and speech and silence reflect the group wisdom process represented by the collection as a whole rather than the contradictory views of individual sages.[20] While the sages sought to control and direct the experience of reality out of a concern for social stability, they also attended to it with a "listening heart," an "openness to the world."[21]

This listening heart worked against normative wisdom's becoming a closed system and disempowered groups such as women, the poor, and those outside the covenant community's being permanently silenced; indeed, it contributed to the development of the figure of personified Wisdom. She is an anomaly that results from the sages' realization of the crucial role of women during the postexilic period in the stabilization of community life centered in the family unit. She partly subverts the status quo, in that she gathers together and validates the social roles of a formally voiceless group.

At the same time she also familiarizes hearers with a patriarchal status quo. Personified Wisdom's implied honoring of women's social roles does not constitute real women's access to formal social influence. She familiarizes hearers with a status quo in which women are a voiceless group in three ways: she addresses only young men; in her body of instruction, proverbs crop up that present women in a pejorative light; in her instructions, the choice of human folly is personified in female form, identified closely with sexual bonding with women beyond the covenant community. By the time of the writing of Sirach in the second century B.C.E., personified Wisdom is equated with the Torah, read and interpreted exclusively by male scribes.[22]

Israelite wisdom had a tendency to become a rigid ideology, like any other wisdom of order of its time. The eventual subordination of Woman Wisdom to male-dominated structures of religious access is one evidence of this. Despite the acknowledgment of the limits of human wisdom and the sovereignty of God that punctuate the collection, dominant groups within the wisdom community tended to impose constructs on the world. They had to ignore some of the evidence of their own experience to maintain the vision of order conveyed by much of the sentence wisdom in Proverbs. When that happened, they lost the central insight of Israelite wisdom, namely, that "no degree of mastery of the rules and maxims of wisdom can confer absolute certainty. Life retains a mysterious and incalculable element, and it is precisely in this incalculable area that Yahweh is encountered."[23]

Subversive sages from within the ranks of the wisdom process itself stepped forward at such times, reminding it of its deepest guiding insights. The critiques of Job and Qohelet and Jesus are intra-wisdom critiques, addressed from within the wisdom circle, rather than challenges of "mature skepticism" against a naive and untested optimism.

Theological Norms

The central, organizing theological assumption of Proverbs is that nature and daily human experience are loci for Yahweh's revelatory activity. Yahwistic religion was indebted to two modes of divine revelation. On the one hand, Yahweh had revealed himself through decisive historical interventions still remembered in cultic ceremonies. On the other hand, Yahweh as Creator reveals himself through the natural order.[24] While Israel's sages certainly acknowledged God's saving acts of promise, exodus, election, lawgiving, and wilderness guidance as a crucial realm of revelation, their focus was on nature and human experience as arenas of encounter between God and humankind.

Disdain of wisdom that doesn't explicitly mention Yahweh as secular or humanistic represents an imposition of the modern divorce of sacred from secular realms back into Israelite history. For Israel the experiences of the world were always divine experiences, and experiences of God were always experiences of the world. The world is never experienced as purely secular, as apart from the Lord who controls it and who is revealed in it.[25] This is the gift of divine Wisdom, that her order is discernible in daily life. This is also the call of Wisdom, because she is also an active, lifetime search. So the sages were called to actively evaluate their experience and to express their insights in proverbial form. Wisdom also called them to evaluate proverbs from surrounding cultural groups, to be both instructed by them and, at the same time, compelled to spell out their theological implications for the guidance of the faith community. In many cases, the Israelite sages, rather than subverting common wisdom, affirmed its basic insights in theological terms.[26]

In several instances, mundane wisdom is affirmed by its being set in the theological context of Israel's wisdom tradition. Mundane wisdom itself condemns the one who is wise in his own eyes (*hakam be'enaw;* 12:15; 26:5, 12, 16; 28:11) as a fool. He is the sluggard or the rich man who refuses to heed anyone else's counsel because he claims to know everything already (12:15; 28:26).[27] Israelite wisdom shared with Egyptian and Babylonian wisdom the acknowledgment of the limitations of human knowledge. "Theological wisdom" locates those limitations in the context of Yahweh's freedom and inscrutability, calling being wise in one's own eyes an act of disobedience to Yahweh (3:7), a refusal to heed Yahweh's counsel.[28]

Mundane wisdom extols wisdom as a priceless treasure (2:4). Theological wisdom affirms that this treasure is a divine gift (2:6). Mundane wisdom acknowledges the unpredictability of human experience. "Do not boast about tomorrow, for you do not know what a day may bring" (27:1). Theological wisdom places that unpredictability in the context of Yahweh's governance of human affairs. "The human mind plans the way, but the Lord directs the steps" (16:9).

Contemporary preachers can be instructed by the sages' example in critically evaluating the cultural axioms implied in contemporary proverbs, clarifying, affirming, and at times challenging their assumptions guided by the convictions of our biblical wisdom traditions, as well as by insights from other canonical terrain.

Wisdom rests on a reciprocal relationship between faith and experience. She is on the one hand a divine gift of an order to be discerned and a guiding presence in discerning it. She is, on the other hand, a call to a disciplined, active employment of that gift. This is "the basic paradox of wisdom," that "on the one hand, wisdom is something acquired by discipline and docility, but on the other hand, wisdom is a gift of God."[29]

Within the theological context of the revelatory potential of daily experience, the repertoire of theological norms of proverbs consists of three explicitly stated convictions about wisdom.[30] First, all wisdom, however mundane or unpretentious, comes from Yahweh as a gift to those who will receive it " (2:1ff.).

It follows, then, that in the second place, the fear of the Lord, this willingness to obey divine instruction, is the beginning or prerequisite of knowledge.[31] Injunctions about the "fear of the Lord" punctuate the collection (1:7; 9:10; 15:33; see also Job 28:28 and Ps. 111:10) Fear of the Lord also appears in 31:30 as a kind of conclusion to the book. Fear of the Lord had many meanings in the Hebrew Bible, from the awareness of the gulf between the human and the divine exemplified in Isaiah 6, to the cultic piety of the psalms, to the covenant loyalty of Deuteronomy. Its meaning in Proverbs is the basic recognition that commitment to God is both the motivation for and the ultimate source of insights for daily life gained by observation of natural and human realms.[32]

Wisdom, in the third place, is a body of instruction for the ordering of personal and social life, given revelatory status through the mediation of personified Wisdom, which may be ignored only at one's peril.[33] Wisdom's ordering function spans historical-social, theological, and literary levels. At the historical-social level, she offers proverbs for the ordering of personal and social harmony. At the literary level, she is a unifying literary device, that of personification, which serves to draw into a unity a diverse body of proverbs. Theologically, Wisdom is a religious symbol who mediates between divine and human, offering the gift of a discernible order in creation, summoning hearers to a disciplined search for that order in the challenging situations of daily life.[34]

Proverbs' repertoire of theological norms, that wisdom is a divine gift which begins with fear of the Lord and issues in an ordered personal and social life, make up a "wisdom of order," which contrasts with Jesus' and Qohelet's "wisdom of counter-order."[35] Proverbs' wisdom of order is based on the convictions of the knowability and justice of God's rule in human life. Two pillars that uphold this vision of the ordered life at both personal and social levels are the dichotomy between the wise and the fool and the connection between act and consequence.

Juxtaposed with these affirmations of stability and predictability are proverbs that defamiliarize readers to theological order by highlighting the unpredictability of human experience, the limitations of human knowledge, and the freedom and inscrutability of God. Proverbs recognize that God's ways are often mysterious (30:2–4) and that the way of justice can be perverted by human violence and evil.[36] These proverbs which subvert order within Proverbs temper the potential hubris of the ordering impulse.

Literary Norms

We will first discuss the literary norms of the repertoire of the collection as a whole, then focus on those norms that characterize individual proverbs. A literary meta-norm of Proverbs is the pairing of proverbs with the personification of Wisdom as a female figure. Personification is a literary dynamic that draws specifics up to an abstract, general level. Personified Wisdom draws to herself the qualities and competencies of women in the early postexilic period. Proverbs, on the other hand, have a dispersing function, in that they arise from and seek to be applied in the diverse experiences of daily life. So Woman Wisdom, calling in marketplace, street, and field, draws her proverbs and those who would use them to herself and then sends them out into the highways and by-ways of life together.[37]

The literary norms of the Proverbs collection bespeak a quest for order clarified by means of comparisons and contrasts that express the dependability of the universe and encourage those qualities within the human community. The book of Proverbs' architectural formulas, by means of comparison and contrast, express an ordered vision of the world and shape conduct consistent with it. Equational forms assert analogies between the realm of nature and human relationships, whereas oppositional forms point up discrepancies between what is wise and what is foolish. Several forms of poetic parallelism, typical of Hebrew poetry, embody these insights.

Equational Proverbs

The *synonymous parallelism* is a proverb type composed of two de-scriptive elements (topic-comment units) in which the architectural formula (relationship between the two units) is equational. The sec-ond unit emphasizes the moral of the first. This is what is called *elab-oration,* where the second descriptive element (topic-comment unit) intensifies the thought of the first or extends it in time. Synonymous parallelism is the primary form of proverbs in Proverbs 16—22.[38]

> By wisdom a house is built, and by understanding it is established. (24:3)

> Wise warriors are mightier than strong ones, and those who have knowledge than those who have strength. (24:5)

A *comparative proverb* is a type of equational proverb in which some aspect of the realm of nature is related, by analogy, to some aspect of human behavior.

> Like a dog that returns to its vomit is a fool who reverts to his folly. (Prov. 26:11)

> Like the glaze covering an earthen vessel are smooth lips with an evil heart. (26:23)

> Like vinegar to the teeth, and smoke to the eyes, so are the lazy to their employers. (10:26)

Like the cold of snow in the time of harvest are faithful messengers to those who send them. (25:13)

This form is especially prominent in chapters 25—26.

Oppositional Proverbs

Antithetical parallelism is the primary form of proverbs in chapters 10—15. The form of this type of proverb is a multidescriptive element (two topic-comment units) in which the architectural formula (relationship between the two units) is contrastive or oppositional. Their function is to expose folly by contrasting it with its wise opposites, on subjects ranging from parental guidance to the control of the tongue, false balances, laziness, gossip, anxiety, and hope deferred.

> The mouth of the righteous brings forth wisdom, but the perverse tongue will be cut off. (Prov. 10:31)

> Those who guard their mouths preserve their lives; those who open wide their lips come to ruin. (Prov. 13:3)

"Better than" proverbs *(Ṭôb-Sprüche)* are a form that is interspersed throughout the book of Proverbs.[39] A remarkable similarity of themes and vocabulary exists between the "better than" proverbs of Amenemope and Proverbs 10—22. They include poverty, quietness, self-control, and the moral superiority of wisdom and poverty to folly and power. In both collections, "better than" proverbs often function as introductory or concluding devices in longer units. On the surface, they look like comparisons (something is better than something else), but they function more like antitheses. They take up two sharply opposed choices, one of which is clearly good and the other not to be chosen. Their form is a single descriptive element (one topic-comment unit) in which the architectural formula (relationship between the topic and the comment) is contrastive.

Two literary norms are conspicuously absent in Proverbs as compared with Qohelet and the Synoptic Jesus. One is literary paradox, which places two opposites side by side and equates them, teasing the hearer into discerning in what situations they can be equated. "Whoever would save his life will lose it, and whoever loses his life will find it." A couple of proverbs observe paradoxes in human behavior (26:27; 11:24), but they do not undercut the wise-fool polarities of antithetical proverbs, which place wisdom and folly side by side and give a clear nod to wisdom. The job of using paradox to undermine conventional norms is left to Qohelet and the Synoptic Jesus. The other literary norm rare in Proverbs is the impossible question. Proverbs abounds in rhetorical questions, useful in didactic settings, which beg an obvious answer any fool can provide! "Can fire be carried in the bosom without burning one's clothes?" (6:27). Impossible questions, which abound in Job, Ecclesiastes, and the Synoptic sayings, are those which have no satisfactory answer, whose purpose is to point to the limits of human knowledge and the sovereignty of God.[40]

5

Increasing Knowledge Increases Sorrow: Biblical Proverbs That Subvert Order

cclesiastes contains a number of proverbial sayings. They fall into two camps, which at first glance seem to be mutually exclusive. Some affirm the value of a wisdom of order, affirming its equation of life with good fortune and the causal link between wise acts and auspicious outcomes (7:5, 6; 8:1, 12; 10:2, 8, 9, 10, 12). Other sayings and comments subvert those same norms, highlighting facts of life that are only alluded to in Proverbs: the suffering of the wise and the prosperity of fools (8:14), the oppression of the powerless (4:1, 2), the fragility of wisdom in the face of folly (9:18; 10:1), and the imminence of death for the wise just as surely as for the fool (2:16f; 9:2).

QOHELET'S SUBVERSIVE PROVERBS AND APHORISMS

Scholars have done much brow-furrowing over these two apparently contradictory groups of proverbial sayings and have come up with several theories to explain away the contradictions between them. Some argue that the book is a disputation between rival wisdom schools, others that the subversive sayings are later interpolations into the book. The best explanation for the two types of sayings attributes them to Qohelet himself, from his own conflicting impulses.[1] On the one hand he wished to affirm traditional wisdom tenets as a guide to life's experiences, and so he crafted or perhaps borrowed traditional-sounding proverbial sayings. On the other hand, his own experience and observation told him that many situations in life subvert traditional wisdom's orderly depiction of the benefits of wisdom and the dangers of folly. This led him to make observations in aphoristic form that subvert the tenets of traditional wisdom.[2]

Qohelet's subversive use of proverbs and aphorisms does not spring from his desire to rebel against his tradition. Rather, it is a poignant admission that life itself subverts the traditional wisdom he views as the way life ought to be. Qohelet's critique of normative wisdom is an intra-wisdom critique, in continuity with the subversive seeds implicit in the wisdom process, already noted in Proverbs: the acknowledgment of the limitations of human wisdom and the inscrutability of God.

In Ecclesiastes, "it is wisdom herself, by her own strength and with her own weapons, which is correcting her own principles. In this perspective one can see the wisdom movement as continuing the emphasis on the limitations of wisdom which were certainly experienced and also articulated all along the way."[3]

Qohelet's use of proverbial sayings draws on several subversive tactics. Sometimes he employs a traditional-sounding proverb, perhaps borrowed, perhaps of his own devising, and uses it to make a point that subverts the point it is used to make in traditional wisdom.(1:15, 18) Still other times he places contrasting observations side by side (8:12–14).

At other times he employs aphorisms, probably of his own devising, that invest the proverbial form with subversive content (for example, the series of "better than" sayings in chapter 7). He coins these aphorisms out of just the kinds of situations that are ignored or suppressed by normative wisdom, and they are often bitter reversals of normative wisdom's definitions of value and life. Even at their most bitter, Qohelet's subversive aphorisms spring from his positive valuation of normative wisdom and his disillusionment that the way things are is not the way they ought to be. Qohelet allows the inscrutability of God, the inequities of daily life, and the imminence of death to subvert normative wisdom, destroying the link between act and consequence and the relevance of the wise-fool dichotomy.

The following sayings from Ecclesiastes conform to the syntactic, semantic, and pragmatic properties of a proverb.[4]

> *One-phrase equational proverbs:* 4:5; 7:9b; 10:4b. For example, "Calmness will undo great offenses" (10:4b).

Synonymous parallelism: 1:15; 3:1; 5:3; 7:7, 11, 12, 19; 8:1b; 10:3, 8, 9, 15, 18; 11:4. "What is crooked cannot be made straight, and what is lacking cannot be counted" (1:15).

Comparative proverbs (Similitudes): 7:6; 10:1, 10; 11:3. "Dead flies make the perfumer's ointment give off a foul odor; so a little folly outweighs wisdom and honor" (10:1).

Oppositional proverbs: "A threefold cord is not quickly broken" (4:12b).

Antithetical parallelism: 2:14, 26; 4:11; 5:12; 7:4, 29; 10:2, 12. "The wise have eyes in their head, but fools walk in darkness" (2:14).

"Better than" proverbs: 2:13; 4:2, 3, 6, 9, 13; 5:1, 5; 6:9; 7:1, 2, 3, 5, 8; 9:4, 16, 17, 18. "It is better to hear the rebuke of the wise than to hear the song of fools" (7:5).

"There is nothing better than" proverbs: 2:24; 3:12, 22; 8:15. "There is nothing better for mortals than to eat and drink, and find enjoyment in their toil" (2:24).

Paradoxical proverbs: 1:15; 1:18; 7:4. "For in much wisdom is much vexation, and those who increase knowledge increase sorrow" (1:18).

Impossible questions: 2:16, 22; 3:21, 22b; 5:11; 6:11–12. "What do mortals get from all the toil and strain with which they toil under the sun?" (2:22).

NORMS OF PROVERBIAL SAYINGS IN QOHELET

Historical-Social Norms

The opening words of Ecclesiastes introduce the work as a collection of the teachings of Qohelet, whose name probably means "Gatherer,"/"Collector," or "Compiler" from the Hebrew *qāhāl,* "assembly."[5] He identifies himself as "king in Jerusalem," an allusion to Solomon that tips us off that this work is a parody of ancient Near Eastern royal inscriptions, works that recount the great deeds of kings of the past.

In reality Qohelet was a sage, probably writing in Palestine in the fifth century B.C.E. The Persian period during which he taught was a time of rapid economic, political, and social change. A growing market economy combined with a system of Persian royal favoritism created a milieu of unique opportunities for common people, but unpredictable risks as well. Persian kings gave land grants (portions) to their favorites, fostering a wide gap between society's fortunate and less fortunate. A changing economy brought ordinary citizens opportunities to borrow, invest, and advance, but also exposed them to the risks of loans, mortgages, and foreclosures. Ordinary folk lived at the mercy of provincial judges, rich proprietors, and other powerful officials who circumvented the law for their own benefit (chap. 5). Qohelet's audience consisted of middle-class working people, neither rich nor poor, homesteaders, perfumers (10:1), quarry workers, woodcutters, hunters, and farmers. Their daily routines involved the constant possibility of accidents and death (10:8–9). For these people there was much to worry about, and little to be certain about (Seow, 1:77–89).

In coping with the situation, Qohelet's audience tried many approaches: they toiled, fretted, were never content with what they had, accumulated wealth and hoarded it, longed for more wisdom and understanding, tried to give an account of all that was happening, desired to straighten out all that was crooked, and/or strove for immortality through fame, wealth, or accomplishments (Seow, 2:138). In the context of so precarious a world, Qohelet subverts the assurances of conventional wisdom and the preoccupations they foster: discontent and envious toil. He offers a new preoccupation: the enjoyment of God's gift of joy in tending one's portion, no matter how small.

Qohelet's wisdom represents a unique response to the trying historical times of the postexilic period, when God became thought of as increasingly remote. Normative wisdom struggled to maintain its confidence in an ordered world and to inculcate proverbial norms of orderly social behavior to keep the postexilic community stable. Some circles of prophecy and wisdom responded to their historical subjection by foreign powers by moving in an apocalyptic direction.[6] They urged the exiles not to remember the former things because God was about to do "a new thing," (Isa. 43:18–19). God would bring from nowhere a new thing, previously unheard of and unknown (Isa. 48:7). In other circles, older, practical wisdom based on observation of daily experience in the present shifted toward wisdom defined as secrets of the end time mediated through angelic figures to apocalyptic sages. There was a proliferation of intermediary figures in some circles of Jewish faith, in the form of both angels and hyposta-tized entities.[7] Qohelet represents a unique voice in this panoply of responses to community turmoil and the perception of a distant God. He continues in traditional wisdom's focus on the present as the source of inductive insights useful for daily life, rather than on wisdom as apocalyptic secrets whose revelation is necessary for interpreting coming events. He challenges apocalyptic's anticipation of something new, asserting: "What has been is what will be, and what has been done is what will be done; there is nothing new under the sun" (1:9).[8] He reports his perambulatory observations that lead him to the conclusion that the vision of order of normative wisdom is continuously being subverted by the inequities of daily life. While Qohelet laments the absurdity of human life under a distant, inscrutable God, at the same time he repeatedly advocates embracing the limited possibilities of human life as good, if precarious, gifts from God (2:24; 3:12, 22; 8:15).

Qohelet's use of proverbs and aphorisms constitutes a type of subversive teaching whose goal was to undermine the certitudes of the existing order rather than to suggest a counter-order way of life. Qohelet's subversive outlook considered substantial social change to be impossible.[9]

Jesus' subversive sayings not only undercut but posit a new, though not fully realized, social order, one that calls for its own code of behavior (e.g., the "kingdom of God" in Q and Luke). The new order is either to be more egalitarian or to grant power and position to certain social groups from whom they have been withheld.[10]

Qohelet's proverbial sayings represent an order-undermining, intermediary step between the order-inculcation of Proverbs and the counter-order of the Synoptic sayings.[11]

Theological Norms

An Encounter between Human Beings and a Mysterious God

The theological meta-norm of sayings in Proverbs was that nature and experience were realms of divine revelation. In the background is a recognition of the limits of human wisdom and a degree of divine inscrutability, but in the foreground is a confidence in access to the divine will via the gift of wisdom mediated through the created order. Qohelet places the mystery of God and human limitations in the foreground and the knowability of God via wisdom in the background. Qohelet presents us with a theological anthropology, a depiction of an unpredictable life lived out in the context of an inscrutable God responsible for enjoyment and injustice alike, who is to be revered and not challenged. "For God is in heaven, and you upon earth; therefore let your words be few" (5:2) (Seow, 2:133–38).

The theological meta-norm for Qohelet is that human observation and experience is the realm of encounter between human beings and the mysterious and, indeed, mystifying, "work of God" (8:17). Qoheleth's God is the God of Israel, the creator (12:1), who has made everything "suitable for its time" (3:11). But a sense of the inscrutability of this God looms large for Qohelet, which helps explain his consistent use of the generic name *ĕlōhîm* instead of the sacred name YHWH.[12] YHWH is the name for the God of the covenant, the God of Israel, whereas *ĕlōhîm* is the universal term for the deity, the God of the universe and of every person. Qohelet's God is transcendent and inscrutable, quite present and active in the cosmos, giving and doing, but never, unlike YHWH, speaking or dealing directly with individuals or nations.[13]

Qohelet parts company both with traditional wisdom and with the rest of the Hebrew scriptures in his views of the "work of God." For Qohelet the "work of God" is neither the placement of a discernible order in creation, nor a series of saving acts punctuating Israel's history. Rather, the term refers to the simultaneously revealing and concealing activity of God as human beings encounter it in the realm of shared human experiences. Those experiences include the various times that meet a person (3:1–8), one's toil (2:18–23; 6:7–9), the uncertainty of riches (5:9–16), the reality of oppression (4:1–3), and the ugly fact of death (2:11–17; 3:19–21). Human beings cannot know the work of God, but only encounter its mysterious and mystifying reality.[14]

Despite all human efforts, human beings are unable to find out all God's work that is done under the sun (8:17). The inscrutability of the work of God is compared with human ignorance of gestation (11:5). Elsewhere, it is attributed to divine agency. God has put a sense of past and future *(hā'ōlām)* in the human heart, so that human beings will be conscious of and yearn for that which transcends the present; and yet, at the same time, God has set limits that frustrate that yearning (3:11).[15]

The work of God is something God has made crooked and no one can straighten out (7:13; 1:15). The work of God describes the mysterious manifestations of God's activity that affect all of human life.[16]

Wisdom as Portion

Proverbs is characterized by three explicit theological norms: that wisdom is a gift from God, that the fear of the Lord is the beginning of the search for wisdom, and that living by wisdom leads to a certain order of personal and social life. The theological reflections that underly Qohelet's use of proverbial sayings manage to subvert all three of normative wisdom's assumptions.

The first theological norm noted in Proverbs is that wisdom is a gift of God, expressed by means of personified Wisdom. For Qohelet, wisdom is not a gift in the sense of being an encompassing order of personal and social life, the search for which leads to life and preserves one from death. In Proverbs, while folly, personified as a woman, stalks her unsuspecting prey, Woman Wisdom walks the highways of everyday life, calling, stretching out her hands, making accessible her gift of wisdom which saves one from the path of folly. Qohelet depicts himself as being chased by Woman Folly even as he is desperately seeking an elusive Wisdom, who alone can deliver him from Folly's grasp, but is not to be found (7:23–26) (Seow, 2:167).

Qohelet subverts the notion that following Wisdom's path of industry and abstemiousness leads to long life, weighty reputation, riches, and honor. Qohelet repeatedly severs the pursuit of wisdom from profit (*yitrôn*) (2:13, 14) and equates its pursuit with *hebel* (1:17, 18). It has value in relation to folly (2:13f.; 7:11–12), but there is no profit in its pursuit, since death comes to wise and fool alike, and with death comes the eradication of knowledge (2:13ff.). Nor is there any profit in toil, for everything goes on in a wearisome cycle and nothing is remembered (1:2–11; 2:11)[17]

There may be no profit to be gained, but nevertheless there is a gift to be found. Says Qohelet, "Moreover, it is God's gift that all should eat and drink and take pleasure in all their toil" (3:13). "So I saw that there is nothing better than that all should enjoy their work, for that is their lot [*hēleq*].[18] Who can bring them to see what will be after them?" (3:22). The word meaning lot or portion occurs several times in the book (2:10, 21; 3:22; 5:18; 9:6, 9). The word can be used to refer concretely to an assigned plot of land or an inheritance, probably inspired, in Qohelet's thinking, by the Persian kings' system of land grants. Understood metaphorically, it is a reference to "the space allotted for human existence." Life is an inherited lot that one works, which holds both the inevitable reality of toil and the possibility of enjoyment. Joy in the midst of toil is the human portion.[19] Wisdom's gift for Qohelet is recognizing and embracing life's limited possibilities, grasping the opportunity that each moment's experience bears as both a precious and a precarious gift.[20]

Fear God! A Response to Human Limitations

The second theological norm of Proverbs, for which Qohelet has a subversive version, is that the fear of the Lord is the beginning of wisdom. Qohelet does not use the term, common to the rest of the Bible, "the fear of the Lord/God," but rather he admonishes one to "fear God!"[21] In Qohelet, the admonition to "fear God!" is more a reaction to the unknowability of God in human experience than, as it is in Proverbs, the starting point for the search for wisdom's ordered life via the created realm.[22] Qohelet's understanding of the term *the fear of God* reflects the older view of awe in the face of the numinous, recognition of the gulf between the human and the divine. For Qohelet this was the painful message of the continual frustration of wisdom's expectations by the realities of daily life.[23] To fear God is the only appropriate response to the God of Qohelet's understanding, for several reasons. God's ways are mysterious (3:11). God is a far-off and unapproachable being to Qohelet, who disposes of the determined times at the divine pleasure (3:1–8). Life and death depend on this God who causes happiness and calamities, in whose hand are power, weakness, and social institutions (3:1–15). These events are not examples of God's retribution; they are simply God's acts.

God desires awe as a human response, instilling humans with a desire to search for order and, at the same time, frustrating that search, "so that all should stand in awe before him" (3:14). For many reasons, then, Qohelet believes that a healthy measure of fear of God ranks higher than justice or wisdom (see also 5:6; 7:18).[24]

Hebel:
Subversion of Conventional Wisdom

A third theological norm of Proverbs is that wisdom is based on and leads to a discernible order of personal and social life. In proverbial wisdom, the one who found wisdom found life (8:35–36). Qohelet offers the subversive version of the ordered life when he says that "All is vanity"(1:2; 12:8). He punctuates his collection with this assertion, marking the end of discrete units with the judgments "all is *hebel*," or "that, too, is *hebel*." The Hebrew word *hebel,* which is often translated as "vanity," has no true English equivalent. The literal meaning of hebel is breath or breeze.[25] The literal sense is relatively uncommon in the Bible. Rather, the Hebrew word is most frequently used as a metaphor for anything that is unreliable or incongruous, whether that thing is fleeting, ephemeral, evanescent, insignificant, worthless, superficial, ridiculous, farcical, unpredictable, or just uncertain. That which is *hebel* is ultimately unpredictable and beyond human ability to control.[26]

Qohelet uses *hebel* specifically of human existence and experience of earthly realities, and not of God or of the cosmos in general. The nuances of the word vary from text to text, with no single definition working in every case. Qohelet uses *hebel* to speak of the ephemerality of life (6:12; 7:15; 9:9), as something of little consequence (5:7; 6:4, 11), joy (2:1), human accomplishments (2:11; 4:4), and youth and the prime of life (11:10) (Seow, 3:258).

Basic to Qohelet's thinking are certain assumptions about the way reality *should* operate. The universe should be reasonable in its workings. His primary assumption is his legacy from traditional proverbial wisdom: that wise actions should lead to positive consequences and foolish ones to negative consequences. At the same time that he holds on to this expectation, his own observation and experiences subvert it, pointing out that no such reasonableness exists, no "as the crow flies" path is paved between cause and effect. His expectations are constantly frustrated.[27]

Qohelet expresses his disappointment with experience for its failure to compensate wisdom for its excellence by calling everything *hebel. Hebel* is not incomprehensibility, in the sense that one cannot know something or it has no meaning; rather, *hebel* describes something that is characterized by an active violation of meaningfulness.[28] For example, it is *hebel,* absurdity, that, while wisdom excels folly as light excels darkness (2:13), the wise person dies and is forgotten just like the fool.

"The essence of the absurd is a disparity between two phenomena that are supposed to be joined by a link of harmony or causality but are actually disjunct or even conflicting. The absurd is irrational, an affront to reason, in the broad sense of the human faculty that seeks and discovers order in the world about us. The quality of absurdity does not inhere in a being, act, or event in and of itself (though these may be, by extension, called absurd), but rather in the tension between a certain reality and a framework of expectations"(Fox, 31).

Qohelet both makes the thematic statement that everything is *hebel*, and applies the term in analyzing several specific situations (35). The origins of *hebel*, the root of what makes human striving absurd, lie in the fact that God has instilled in human beings the yearning to know the plans of God from start to finish *('ōlām)*, and yet their desire is frustrated by God himself (3:9ff.). Death cuts one off forever from all hope of *'ōlām*, it forecloses the hope of further knowledge and the remembrance of that knowledge one has attained in life.[29] In conventional wisdom the intelligent seek knowledge and the fool pursues folly (Prov. 15:14). Irony abounds in Qohelet's depiction of the consummate wise king (Solomon) as engaged in the search for wisdom which turns out to be "but a chasing after wind" (1:17).[30]

The two pillars of traditional wisdom's ordered world are the act-consequence sequence and the wise-fool dichotomy. *Hebel* expresses the fact that the deed and consequence have divorced, sweeping away traditional wisdom's grounds for commending wisdom over folly (2:14; 2:16; 6:8,11).[31]

Literary Norms

Qohelet presents his work as a parody of the literary genre of royal propaganda literature called the royal inscription, common in the ancient Near East, in which a king introduces himself and boasts of his achievements, wisdom, and wealth as superior to his predecessors and a legacy for posterity. Qohelet presents himself in 1:12 as one who has been king over Israel in Jerusalem, a clear allusion to Solomon, but his work is a subversive version of the royal inscription genre. This is evident in the fact that this king's achievement is to discover that kings, however wise, have no advantage over fools and to recognize that his legacy to posterity is to be forgotten.[32]

Qohelet's use of proverbs and aphorisms is designed to draw readers into an experience of the subversion of traditional wisdom that motivates his royal inscription. He uses them to give the impression of making a particular point, but then the first impression quickly dissipates like mist, and one is led to a different conclusion (Seow 2:1, 2). This pattern of "literary setups" involves the reader in an experience of *hebel*—the act of reading becomes a chasing after wind. This is a graphic example of the defamiliarization that is an essential dynamic of profound literature: the reader is led to repeatedly question assumptions about reality he or she has up until now viewed as givens.

In exploring the literary norms that contribute to Qohelet's subversive use of proverbs, one must look at two levels: proverbs *as* texts, and proverbs *in* texts. That is to say, one must look at their discrete form and content *and* at the impact that their literary context has on them.

Proverbs (or Aphorisms) as Subversive Texts

In Ecclesiastes one encounters the same basic relationships between the proverbs' topic and comments that one has already encountered in the book of Proverbs: the equational or identificational and the oppositional or contrastive. In the proverbs of the book of Proverbs, equational forms are synonymous parallelism and comparative proverbs. Oppositional forms are antithetical parallelism and "better than" *(Ṭôb-Spruch)* proverbs. We noted the predominance of antithetical parallelism, which built an ordered world by maximizing the differences between wisdom and folly in specific patterns of thought and behavior, presenting the former as the clear choice for those who desire life. We noted the paucity of paradoxical proverbs, literal proverbs that juxtapose seeming opposites and thereby undercut commonly held assumptions.

Here in Qohelet, one finds synonymous parallelism, similitudes, and antithetical parallelism. While he places sayings in contexts that subvert their adequacy, at the level of content of individual proverbs one hears in several places an echo of Proverbs' affirmation of a discernible pattern of behavior called wisdom that is preferable to folly.

> Wisdom is as good as an inheritance, an advantage to those who see the sun. (7:11) *(synonymous parallelism)*
> Wisdom gives strength to the wise more than ten rulers that are in a city. (7:19) *(synonymous parallelism)*
> The wise have eyes in their head, but fools walk in darkness. (2:14) *(antithetical parallelism)*

> Wisdom makes one's face shine, and the hardness of
> one's countenance is changed. (8:1) *(synonymous
> parallelism)*
> The heart of the wise inclines to the right, but the heart
> of a fool to the left. (10:2) *(antithetical parallelism)*[33]

Qohelet's aphorisms/proverbs display the subversive impulse that
is an undercurrent in the proverbial wisdom of Proverbs, the acknowledgment of the limitations of human wisdom in the face of
divine inscrutability and freedom. This subversive impulse is emphasized in four types of proverbs in Qohelet: "better than" *(Ṭôb-
Spruch)* proverbs, paradoxical proverbs, impossible questions, and a
type of proverb unique to Qohelet, the "nothing is better than"
proverb.

"Better than" Proverbs (Ṭôb-Sprüche). The "better than"
proverbs interspersed throughout the book of Proverbs take up two
sharply opposed choices, one of which is clearly good, the other
clearly not to be chosen. They commend certain kinds of conduct as
clearly superior to others. Several of Qohelet's "better than" proverbs
serve the same function, confirming normative wisdom's depiction of
what is wisdom and what is folly in the ordered life.[34]

Qohelet modifies the traditional "better than" proverb by invest-
ing its traditional form with tradition-subverting subject matter. One
focus of his "better than" sayings is the vulnerability of wisdom to the
folly of fools: "Wisdom is better than weapons of war, but one bungler destroys much good" (9:18).

References to death in Proverbs usually connect it with folly
(13:14), loose women (2:16–19), and ignoring, even hating wisdom's
precepts (8:36). Death is that which can be avoided by adhering to
values of righteousness and wisdom (10:2; 11:4; 14:27; 21:6).

In a strange subversion of traditional counsel to avoid death, Qohelet asserts that death is preferable to life, because it is a welcome escape from having to observe the injustices and sufferings to which so
many are subjected in this life (4:2). He does not, like Lamentations
and Job, hold God culpable for oppression; rather, injustice is a fact
of life, something everyone who is alive sees.[35]

Death, the status of being a stillborn child who enters the transient
world devoid of consciousness and sight, is preferable to the condi-

tion of the living who, while they have a choice to see good as well as evil, spend their lives complaining (6:3) (Seow, 4:511–12).

Life lived in enjoyment of the precious, yet precarious, opportunities of the present moment, however, is vastly preferable to death. "A living dog is better than a dead lion" (9:4). The contrast is filled with irony, because the dog was among the most despised creatures in the ancient Near East, while the lion was the most admired of creatures (Seow, 6:647). "But better than both is the one who has not yet been, and has not seen the evil deeds that are done under the sun" (4:3).

In chapter 7 Qohelet uses a series of "better than" proverbs in an extended rhetoric of subversion of the whole notion that the wise are qualified to advise others on what is *ṭôb* (good or better) for humanity. "For who knows what is good for mortals while they live the few days of their vain life, which they pass like a shadow?"(6:12). He presents a series of traditional-sounding wisdom sayings in dialectical pairs, contrasting birth and death (verse 1b), funeral and wedding (2), merriment and sadness (3), mourning and pleasure (4), rebuke and praise (5), the wise and the fool (6), beginning and end (8a), patience and arrogance (8b). In almost every case, Qohelet follows the traditional-sounding tenet with a statement that forces it to an absurd conclusion and thereby undercuts its authority as wise advice. For example, the traditional notion that a good name is to be cherished because it lives on after one's death is pushed to the absurd conclusion that "the day of death [is therefore better] than the day of birth," and that, further, "It is better to go to the house of mourning than to go to the house of feasting" (7:2). The passage is intentionally confusing, its wisdom asserted, then subverted, like vapor, evaporating away. The undermining of one statement with another is a typical method employed in ancient Near Eastern pessimistic literature to show that there is no real solution to life's contradictions. As Choon-Leong Seow points out, "All in all, we must see 7:1–12 as a parody of the verbosity of all those who readily dish out advice as to what is good and tell other people what they should do in every situation" (5:538).

***"There is nothing better than"* proverbs.** Another proverbial form Qohelet employs is the "there is nothing better than" proverb, one that may be unique to him. He punctuates his first-person account of his observation of the inequities of life with this proverbial type. It appears

four times in Qohelet, in explicit connection with the theme of enjoyment (2:24; 3:12–13, 22; and 8:15). "There is nothing better for mortals than to eat and drink, and find enjoyment in their toil" (2:24). Each
example of the form is followed by a clause that relates the advice to
the divine intention for human enjoyment.[36]

The "there is nothing better" saying constitutes "an animated affirmation . . . that man [sic] has no higher good than to synchronize
with this divine intention"(Ogden, 341). "Here for the first time,
Qohelet is aware that he is in accord with the divine purpose; here
he sees himself face to face with a beneficent God."[37]

In context, three out of the four examples (2:24; 3:12; and 8:15)
summarize the author's reaction to the *hebel* situation that he has out-
lined in the preceding section. In 2:18ff. the *hebel* situation is that people toil a lifetime only to leave their wealth to others. In 3:1ff., Qohelet
laments the fact that God both places within human beings the desire
for wisdom and knowledge and continually frustrates that desire. And
in 8:14 Qohelet describes the situation that neither wicked nor righteous behavior is compensated in accordance with the expectations of
normative wisdom.

The function of the "there is nothing better" saying is to express the
advice to enjoy life in light of Qohelet's negative response to the question that is programmatic for his thought: "What do people gain . . . ?"
(1:3). There is no profit, but there is a portion (Ogden, 350).

In two of the four instances of "there is nothing better" sayings,
the saying is immediately preceded by the "What does it profit?"
question, and together the two provide the literary framework for the
text in which they are placed (2:22; 3:9) (350). In 8:15 the "there is
nothing better" saying is immediately followed by the explanatory
clause that enjoyment helps people persevere in the "toil through the
days of life that God gives them under the sun." The "there is nothing better" saying proves to be the vehicle for the theological norm
of *ḥēleq,* which Qohelet affirms despite the severance of profit from
toil and the pursuit of wisdom.

Paradoxical proverbs. The paradox, which was infrequent in
Proverbs, is more abundant in Qohelet. What is viewed as undesirable by normative wisdom is at times given positive connotations,
while what is viewed favorably by normative wisdom is given negative connotations. Thereby habitual assumptions are undercut and begin to seem strange to the reader/hearer.

For in much wisdom is much vexation, and those who increase
knowledge increase sorrow. (1:18)

The day of death [is better] than the day of birth. (7:1b)

The heart of the wise is in the house of mourning, but the heart of
fools is in the house of mirth. (7:4)

Impossible questions. A type of proverb that occurs in a few places
in the Proverbs, but more frequently in Qohelet, Job, and the Synoptic sayings is the "impossible question."[38] This is a blatantly subversive proverbial form, pointing to the limits of human knowledge
and the inscrutability of God.[39]

How can the wise die just like fools? (2:16)

What do mortals get from all the toil and strain with which they toil
under the sun? (2:22)

Who knows whether the human spirit goes upward and the spirit of
animals goes downward to the earth? (3:21)

The more words, the more vanity, so how is one the better? (6:11)

For who knows what is good for mortals while they live the few days
of their vain life, which they pass like a shadow? (6:12)

Who can make straight what he has made crooked? (7:13)

That which is, is far off, and deep, very deep; who can find it out?
(7:24)

For what advantage have the wise over fools? (6:8)[40]

Proverbs (or Aphorisms) in
Subversive Literary Contexts

Qohelet employs three strategies in his sayings placement that en-
hance their subversive import. One is the use of a traditional proverbial saying followed by an appeal to experience that subverts it. This
is what some scholars have referred to as Qohelet's "yes, but" strategy, in which he gives a statement of traditional wisdom and then
modifies it.[41]

In 2:13–14, Qohelet quotes two traditional-sounding commendations of wisdom as superior to folly. "Wisdom excels folly as light excels darkness. The wise have eyes in their head, but fools walk in
darkness." He subverts these sayings by appealing to his observation

that both wise person and fool die and are forgotten. This is yet another example of *hebel* (2:17). Other examples of Qohelet's "yes, but" strategy appear in 4:9–12; 5:9f.; 8:2–4; 8:5–6; 8:11–14.[42]

A second subversive tactic is to commend a traditional wisdom tenet, but for reasons that reflect his own unique outlook, subverting the saying's traditional meaning. In 1:15, Qohelet is probably quoting a traditional saying used by wisdom teachers to describe the deficiency of certain students who would not or could not learn. ("What is crooked cannot be made straight, and what is lacking cannot be counted.") He uses this traditional saying to make a subversive point: that even the wise cannot straighten out the world in all its perversity and disorder. Experience itself holds a deficiency: it yields order and meaning neither to wise nor to fools, so the wise are really no better off than fools (Seow, vol. 3, 339–41).

In 1:18, Qohelet quotes a proverb that may well have been quoted by wisdom teachers to their students as a sort of ancient version of the "no pain, no gain" proverb: "For in much wisdom is much vexation, and those who increase knowledge increase sorrow." Its traditional meaning is that intellectual achievement does not come without discipline and discomfort. Qohelet quotes it, but in order to make the subversive point that pain is not a means to an end, that of greater wisdom, but rather, pain and trouble are the very results of wisdom. The more one knows, the more painful life can be (vol. 3, 342–43).

A third subversive strategy is the juxtaposition of two proverbial sayings that offer varying interpretations, known as "contrasting proverbs." This is the prophetic use of proverbs, which I have labeled "dueling proverbs," which has precedent in the book of Proverbs itself (26:4, 5). The book of Job also uses this strategy (Job 12:12, 13; 32:7, 8).[43]

In 4:5, 6 Qohelet juxtaposes two proverbs or aphorisms that offer differing interpretations on industry and sloth. "Fools fold their hands and consume their own flesh" appears to be a standard condemnation of the folly of sloth. It is followed by "Better is a handful with quiet than two handfuls with toil, and a chasing after wind," which subverts the previous proverb by questioning the absolute value of industry, since it consists in futile toil. Toil is futile, a chasing after wind, one more example of *hebel*.[44]

In 7:12, Qohelet asserts that "the protection of wisdom is like the protection of money, and the advantage of knowledge is that wisdom gives life to the one who possesses it." Not only is this assertion subverted by the negative evaluation of the pursuit of wealth that has already been offered in chapter 5, but it is immediately followed by "Consider the work of God; who can make straight what he has made crooked?" (7:13).

Chapters 9 and 10 contain two sets of contrasting proverbial sayings, either borrowed or coined by Qohelet, on the theme of the fragility of wisdom in the face of folly. Chapter 9:16 serves as a summary to his observation of the poor man whose wisdom saved a city: "Wisdom is better than might; yet the poor man's wisdom is despised, and his words are not heeded."

Ecclesiastes 9:18 states that "Wisdom is better than weapons of war, but one bungler destroys much good." In both instances, the superiority of wisdom over folly is affirmed, but the persistence of folly and its ability to throw wisdom into disarray is given the last word.

Qohelet follows most of his commendations of wisdom in relation to folly with an affirmation of the power of folly or a comment about the conduct of fools. He sees in the wisdom-folly contrast of traditional wisdom not the freedom of people to choose wisdom and obtain life, but the power of folly and fools to negate the gains of wisdom.[45]

Qohelet's sayings constitute a body of subversive commentary on the topics undertaken by normative wisdom, the virtues of toil, the pursuit of wisdom, the superiority of wisdom over folly, and the connection between wisdom and life and folly and death. The situational origins of Qohelet's aphorisms are more explicit than is the case of either the proverbs of the book of Proverbs or the sayings of the Synoptic Jesus. Qohelet explicitly ties many of his aphorisms and his subverted proverbial sayings to his own experience and observation of specific situations. They reflect his unique perspective: an outlook of pessimism about the possibilities for social change, yet offering the positive advice to his hearers to accept both the limitations and opportunities of their portion as a way of being faithful to a mysterious God.

Qohelet's subversive approach to traditional wisdom constitutes a field rich with homiletical potential. Theologically, the Christian preacher may take issue with Qohelet's divine determinism, social passivity, and conviction that death is the end of all things. At the same time, we need to value his respect for the divine mystery and sovereignty, his honesty about the brutality and absurdity of life and the inadequacy of conventional wisdom to meet it. Qohelet has been called "a preacher of joy," and contemporary preachers do well to value his focus on God's gift of joy in our portion in this present moment, leading our people to affirm that, with all their toil, risks, and pain, our lives together are yet places of opportunity and enjoyment.

Qohelet, both for his own day and for ours, offers a compelling model for the way proverbs can subvert aspects of a culture's normative wisdom by attending to situations that it would rather ignore. His sayings are a helpful homiletical searchlight for illuminating those situations in contemporary life that a preacher judges to be ignored or suppressed by the normative wisdom of order of the present age. They offer a helpful tool for challenging conventional wisdom's preoccupations when they are at odds with our understanding of the priorities for human life in light of our faith. He models several strategies: quoting contrasting proverbs; quoting a traditional proverb and offering subversive commentary on it; and coining subversive aphorisms. Qohelet helps us illuminate those contemporary scenarios in which conventional promises that wise living leads to prosperity and good fortune are revealed to be inaccurate and often hurtful words.

6

All Who Exalt Themselves
Will Be Humbled:
Jesus' Subversive Sayings

ur focus here turns to proverbs attributed to Jesus in the Synoptic Gospels, but proverbial sayings appear elsewhere in the New Testament: in John's Gospel and in the Pauline epistles. These have come to light in the past few decades as New Testament studies, like those of the Hebrew scriptures, have promoted wisdom from margin to center of their reflection.

Jesus is depicted in the Synoptic Gospels as uttering wisdom sayings on a variety of subjects. Recent research strongly suggests that some of these wisdom sayings were part of the earliest traditions ascribed to Jesus. This suggestion challenges the New Testament scholarship of a previous generation which insisted that future-directed eschatology, not wisdom, was primary in the Jesus traditions. By this earlier scholarly view, eschatological anticipation was the real core of Jesus' teaching, and wisdom sayings were gradually provided by the early communities to fill the need for commonsense wisdom to cope with an extended present.

SAYINGS FROM THE Q DOCUMENT

Research over the past several years indicates that wisdom occupied as primary a place as eschatology in the early Jesus traditions. Much research has focused on the material used by Matthew and Luke, but largely missing from Mark, that many scholars call the Q document.[1] About a quarter of the wisdom sayings attributed to Jesus in the Synoptic Gospels are found in the Q material.[2] Q differs from the narrative gospels in two ways. It largely consists of sayings, with a few narrative portions, and it includes no tradition of Jesus' crucifixion and resurrection. On the basis of these divergences from the narrative gospel genre, many scholars have regarded Q as a source of raw materials for the narrative gospels with no particular theological focus of its own.[3]

Others have rightly challenged this view of Q as primitive or inferior due to its lack of a master framing narrative and a passion narrative. They have asserted that it represents a discrete genre from the narrative genre which culminated in Jesus' death and resurrection. By this view, with which I concur, Q belongs in the company of a long line of Hebrew wisdom collections that include Proverbs, Ecclesiastes, Sirach, *Pirke Aboth* and the *Gospel of Thomas*. These collections belong to a wisdom genre called "sayings of the sages" (*logoi sophōn*), collections of sayings associated with a particular sage or group of sages.[4]

Q does not presuppose the passion kerygma's sacrificial understanding of the significance of Jesus' death. Rather, it understands Jesus, along with John the Baptist, as an envoy or prophet of the heavenly Sophia (Greek for Wisdom), whose death is the fate of all her authentic prophets throughout the history of Israel.[5] This understanding has precedent in the Wisdom of Solomon and in Deuteronomy. The Wisdom of Solomon, written in the middle of the first century B.C.E., represents the development of wisdom literature just prior to Christianity as it converged with apocalypticism, Israelite salvation history, and Hellenistic philosophy. Wisdom is read back into salvation history as patroness of the patriarchs and prophets who received God's successive revelations in history. She is depicted as protecting and prospering them.[6] Adding impetus to this identification of Jesus as a persecuted prophet of Wisdom is the Deuteronomistic view of the people's history as the repeated rejections of the prophets, until in the end Israel is itself rejected (Robinson, 13).

In verses that are probably from the latest layer of tradition in Q, Jesus is identified with the heavenly Wisdom (Luke 10:21, 22; Matt. 11:25–27). Matthew takes this identification still farther. In 11:19b he reformulates the Q saying "Wisdom is vindicated by her children" to: "Wisdom is vindicated by her deeds." He also takes the late Jewish notion that Wisdom—so often rejected and having no permanent earthly abode—had come to reside in the Torah (Sirach 24) and relates it to the understanding of Jesus as Wisdom (Matt. 11:28–30). Matthew's

Wisdom Christology is also obvious in his editing of Q's "Therefore also the Wisdom of God said, 'I will send them prophets and apostles,'" to a first-person statement of Jesus: "Therefore I send you prophets, sages, and scribes" (Matt. 23:34). Jesus is no longer merely one among many envoys of Wisdom, but is identified with Wisdom herself (10, 11). This identification of Jesus with the heavenly Wisdom helps explain the distinctive Q understanding of Jesus' death. A theme then current in Jewish apocalypticism as characteristic of the last times was the withdrawal of Wisdom to the heavenly sphere. Wisdom is so regularly rejected on earth that she finally returns to heaven (*4 Ezra* 5:10). So in Q, Jesus—as both sage and Wisdom herself—summons, is rejected, and withdraws.

Later reflection placed this Wisdom Christology in the context of apocalyptic Christology's identification of Jesus with the coming Son of Man. Wisdom, having so often sought to win Jerusalem only to be rejected, pronounces this judgment: "Behold, your house is left to you, desolate. And I tell you, you will not see me until you say, 'Blessed is the one who comes in the name of the Lord'" (Luke 13:35/Matt. 23:38–39) (13).

Given the fact that in Q wisdom sayings are prominent and that they are attributed to Jesus, who is associated with the heavenly Wisdom, Q is best read as words of divine Wisdom or her envoys.[7] So Q is not a mere source of raw materials for the narrative gospels, but is itself a gospel, in the sense that it is, like Matthew, Luke, Mark, and John, a theologically-shaped account of the significance of Jesus' life and death.[8] Q's theological, christological focus is the abiding power of Wisdom's sayings in the present life of believers, calling them to the crucial choice to live by her teachings in light of the coming judgment.[9]

Recent study of Q by John Kloppenborg, Arland Jacobson, and others, based on linguistic, thematic, and sociohistorical analysis, points to the probability that Q took shape in stages that reflect the outlooks of the communities within which it circulated.[10] This redactional work has identified two major blocks of material. One block of material, referred to as "sapiential instruction," or Q1, consists in sapiential sayings directed to members of a sectarian Jewish community focusing on motifs of poverty, discipleship, and the kingdom of God. The focus is subversive living in the present.[11] Several blocks of material (Q2) represent a second stage of Christian development, emphasizing apocalyptic motifs, the coming judgment, the urgency of repentance, the impenitence of this generation, and a missionary turn toward the Gentiles.[12] Q depicts a shift from subversive wisdom for life in the present (Q1) to apocalyptic interpretation of the consequences of the rejection of teachings and teacher (Q2).

The shift from Q1 to Q2 represents a shift in the conception of Jesus' identity as well. In Q1 Jesus, along with John the Baptist, is a prophet of Wisdom. In Q2, Jesus is identified both with personified Wisdom the sender of rejected prophets and with the apocalyptic Son of Man coming to judge the world for rejecting the teachings of Wisdom's emissary. This portrayal of Wisdom may well reflect the need of the early communities of Q to legitimize their distinctive message by appeal to an authority superior to their detractors. The cost of ridicule of the group's message is permanent exclusion from the kingdom at the hands of the coming Son of Man. This reflects the Deuteronomistic theme, which is prominent in Q2, of the fateful consequences of rejecting the message of life (Deut. 30:11f.).[13]

Building on too sharp a redaction-critical separation of the wisdom speeches from the apocalyptic announcement of judgment in Q, some scholars have insisted that Jesus was a sage whose focus was countercultural wisdom devoid of the slightest apocalyptic context.[14] Clearly Q is not an apocalypse, because it lacks the narrative description of a visionary's experience typical of that genre. The major component of Q is appropriately categorized as "wisdom speeches," which commend subversive living in the present, but they are set in the context of an apocalyptic worldview.

Two considerations beg the conclusion that, in addition to being a sage, Jesus was also an apocalyptic prophet. One is the widespread presence of apocalyptic sayings in the Synoptic Gospels beyond Q, and the other is the fact that, in many works of late Judaism, despite our contemporary craving for genre purity, wisdom and apocalyptic were intertwined.[15] Jesus' subversive proverbs and aphorisms represented a return to pragmatic wisdom's focus on the present, but probably in light of apocalyptic expectation. The community elaborated and expanded on an extant apocalyptic element in Q's announcements of judgment when they began to experience the rejection of the teachings of their subversive sage.

We do not have to choose between Jesus the apocalyptic prophet and Jesus the sage to faithfully preach Jesus' subversive aphorisms. We are far better occupied appropriating his subversive proverbial sayings to illuminate our engagement with the challenging situations of the present. Their apocalyptic horizon ought to heighten the urgency of accepting those teachings, not distract us from their relevance to the present. We will now look at the aphoristic sayings of Jesus from Q1 and Q2 and beyond them in the Synoptic Gospels, analyzing their historical-social and literary norms (see table 6.1).

Table 6.1
The Seven Clusters of Teachings Known as Q1[16]

---

1. Teachings Attributed to Jesus

   QS 8   On those who are fortunate (Luke 6:20b–21/Matt. 5:3, 6, 4)[17]
   QS 9   On responding to reproach
           (Luke 6:27, 28, 29, 30/Matt. 5:44, 39b, 40, 42)
           (Luke 6:31/Matt. 7:12)
           (Luke 6:32–35/Matt. 5:46–47, 45)

   QS 10   On making judgments
           (Luke 6:36–38/Matt. 5:48; 7:1–2)[18]
           (Luke 6:36/Matt. 5:48)
           (Luke 6:37/Matt. 7:1, 2)

   QS 11   On teachers and students (Luke 6:39/Matt. 15:14) (Luke
           6:40)/Matt. 10:24, 25)
   QS 12   On hypocrisy (Luke 6:41–42/Matt. 7:3–5)
   QS 13   On integrity (Luke 6:43–45/Matt. 7:15–20; 12:33–35)[19]
   QS 14   On practical obedience (Luke 6:46–49/Matt. 7:24–27)

2. Instructions for the Jesus Movement

   QS 21   On becoming a follower of Jesus
           (Luke 9:57/Matt. 8:19, 20)
           (Luke 9:60/Matt. 8:21)
           (Luke 9:61, 62) (Matthew's motives for omitting this verse are
           unclear)

   QS 22   On working for the kingdom of God (Luke 10:2–11, 16)
           (Luke 10:2/Matt. 9:37)
           (Luke 10:3/Matt. 10:16)
           (Luke 10:4/Matt. 10:9, 10)
           (Luke 10:5/Matt. 10:12)
           (Luke 10:6/Matt. 10:13)
           (Luke 10:7)
           (Luke 10:8)
           (Luke 10:9/Matt. 10:7, 8)

(Luke 10:10/Matt. 10:14)
(Luke 10:11/Matt. 10:7)
(Luke 10:16/Matt. 10:40)

3. Confidence in the Father's Care

QS 27   How to pray (Luke 11:2–4/Matt. 6:7–13)
QS 28   Confidence in asking (Luke 11:9–13/Matt. 7:7–11)[20]

4. On Anxiety and Speaking Out

QS 35   On speaking out (Luke 12:2, 3/Matt. 10:26, 27)
QS 36   On fear (Luke 12:4–7/Matt. 10:28–31)

5. On Personal Goods

QS 38   Foolish possessions (Luke 12:13, 14, 16–21)
QS 39   On food and clothing (Luke 12:22–31/Matt. 6:25–33)[21]
QS 40   On heavenly treasure (Luke 12:33, 34/Matt. 6:19–21)

6. Parables of the Kingdom

QS 49   The mustard and the yeast (Luke 13:18–21/Matt. 13:31–33)

7. The True Followers of Jesus

QS 54   On humility (Luke 18:14/Matt. 23:12).
QS 55   The great supper (Luke 14:15–24/Matt. 22:1–14)[22]
QS 56   On the cost of being a disciple (Luke 14:25–27/Matt. 10:37–39)
QS 57   Savorless salt (Luke 14:34, 35/Matt. 5:13)

The Aphorisms of Q1 and Q2

Obviously not all the material in these seven clusters is proverbial or
aphoristic. Embedded in these blocks of Q1 material are a number of
aphorisms, each of which plays a key rhetorical role in its cluster. Each
cluster has at least one. They function within their unit as a core saying around which the unit is built, or on which supporting considerations build. Proverbs are here used the same way they were sometimes used in the book of Proverbs, as the indicative rationale for
clusters of imperative instruction.[23] Below are listed the sayings I am
classifying as aphorisms in Q1 on the left and beneath them, indented,
the imperatives in each cluster that are built on them.[24]

Aphorisms from Q1

Blessed are you who are poor, for yours is the kingdom of God. (Luke 6:20)

Even sinners love those who love them. (Luke 6:32/Matt. 5:47)

Love your enemies, do good to those who hate you, bless those who curse you, pray for those who abuse you. If anyone strikes you on the cheek, offer the other also; and from anyone who takes away your coat do not withhold even your shirt. Give to everyone who begs from you; and if anyone takes away your goods, do not ask for them again. (Luke 6:27–30/Matt. 5:39–44)

With the judgment you make you will be judged. (Matt. 7:2) Do not judge, and you will not be judged.(Luke 6:37/ Matt. 7:1)

Can a blind person guide a blind person? (Luke 6:39/Matt. 15:14)

A disciple is not above the teacher. (Luke 6:40/Matt. 10:24)

*Why do you see the speck in your neighbor's eye, but do not notice the log in your own eye? (Luke 6:41/Matt. 7:3) First take the log out of your own eye, and then you will see clearly to take the speck out of your neighbor's eye.(Luke 6:42/Matt. 7:5)

No good tree bears bad fruit. (Luke 6:43/Matt. 7:18)

Figs are not gathered from thorns, nor are grapes picked from a bramble bush. (Luke 6:44/Matt. 7:16)

*Each tree is known by its own fruit. (Luke 6:44/Matt. 7:16)

Foxes have holes, and birds of the air have nests; but the Son of Man has nowhere to lay his head. (Luke 9:58/Matt. 8:20)

The harvest is plentiful, but the laborers are few. (Luke 10:2/Matt. 9:37) Ask the Lord of the harvest to send out laborers into his harvest. (Luke 10:2b/Matt. 9:38)

For everyone who asks receives, and everyone who searches finds, and for everyone who knocks, the door will be opened. (Luke 11:10/Matt. 7:8) Ask, and it will be given you. (Luke 11:9/Matt. 7:7)

Nothing is covered up that will not be uncovered, and nothing secret that will not become known. (Luke 12:2/Matt. 10:26) Whatever you have said in the dark will be heard in the light. (Luke 12:3/Matt. 10:27)

Of how much more value are you than the birds! (Luke 12:24/Matt. 6:26) Do not fear those who kill the body, and after that can do nothing more. (Luke 12:4/Matt. 10:28)

For life is more than food, and the body more than clothing. (Luke 12:
23/Matt. 6:25)

> Do not worry about your life, what you will eat, or about
> your body, what you will wear." (Luke 12:22/Matt. 6:25)

Where your treasure is, there your heart will be also. (Luke 12:34/
Matt. 6:21)

> Make purses for yourselves that do not wear out, an un-
> failing treasure in heaven, where no thief comes near and
> no moth destroys. (Luke 12:33/Matt. 6:20)

All who exalt themselves will be humbled, but all who humble themselves will be exalted. (Luke 18:14/Matt. 23:12)

Those who try to make their life secure will lose it, but those who lose
their life will keep it. (Luke 17:33/Matt. 10:39)

If salt has lost its taste, how can its saltiness be restored? (Luke 14:34/
Matt. 5:13)

Aphorisms from Q2

> Whoever is not with me is against me, and whoever does not gather
> with me scatters. (Luke 11:23/Matt. 12:30)

> No one after lighting a lamp puts it in a cellar, but on the lampstand
> so that those who enter may see the light. (Luke 11:33/Matt. 5:15)

> If the owner of the house had known at what hour the thief was com-
> ing, he would not have let his house be broken into. (Luke 12:39/
> Matt. 24:43)

> Some are last who will be first, and some are first who will be last.
> (Luke 13:30/Matt. 19:30)

> No slave can serve two masters. (Luke 16:13/Matt. 6:24)

> Where the corpse is, there the vultures will gather. (Luke 17:37/Matt.
> 24:28)

NORMS OF PROVERBIAL
SYNOPTIC SAYINGS

Historical-Social Norms

The controlling historical-social norm of Proverbs' repertoire is the
equation of wisdom's order with life. The effect of the wisdom instruction of Q was to subvert the prevailing social order of Roman

Palestine and to depict a new social reality. This new counter-order is referred to as the "kingdom (reign, rule) of God" and is envisioned in the Synoptic Gospels as both a present reality and a future event. The choice of this term is deliberately polemical, usurping Rome's "good news" of a new, universal empire of which there would be no end.[25]

The Roman empire's imperial domination exploited not only the Jews, but all those living under its colonial rule. Jesus announced God's power of creation and salvation at work envisioning and crafting an alternative world free of hunger, poverty, and domination. This envisioned world was already present in table fellowship, healings, and the domination-free relationships of the Jesus community.[26]

The Roman empire assumed that the means to life must be "brokered," beginning at the top, with a few drops of sustenance trickling down to the bottom. Jesus, by contrast, began at the bottom, with expendables—the beggars, the prostitutes, the blind and disabled—offering them an "unbrokered empire," in which the means to life are offered freely, without condition, around a table open to the unclean, the dispossessed, the shut out.

Jesus' aphorisms apply, not only to political abuses of his day, but also to religious practices that collaborated with them. They subvert a view of God as guarantor of economic security and status. They targeted Judaism's focus on ritual and racial purity as well as the economic inequities that saw landholding high-priestly families, scribes, lawyers, and Pharisees enjoying economic comfort while peasants were impoverished, degraded, and expendable. Jesus' teachings did not advocate a kind of moral fine-tuning that would eventually perfect human society. He offered a radically different notion of how to order human life.[27]

The aphorisms of Q defamiliarize hearers to the validity of many of the conventions that allow a society to operate, such as the principles of retaliation, the orderly borrowing and lending of capital, appropriate treatment of the dead, responsible self-provision, self-defense, and honor of parents.[28] They expose claims to superior status based on such things as wealth, learning, possessions, secrets, rank, and power as questionable, if not ridiculous. Implicit in the critique is the assumption that simplicity is better than pretension, that realistic assessment is a better guide than status, and that compassion is to be preferred to ritual purity. Sympathies lie with the poor, the least, the humble, the servant, the excluded, and those consigned to positions without privilege, more than with their social opposites.[29]

While Q1's instructions are offered on behalf of Palestinian social, economic, and cultural outcasts, they are addressed to those who are on the margins by choice, who have some of the accouterments of the status quo, such as home, money, and family, to give up, not those who lack them in the first place. Only after their countercultural behavior earns them rejection by the status quo does the Q community understand what it means for them to be marginal by other than their own choice.[30]

The aphorisms attributed to Jesus in Q include the critique of hypocrisy and the critique of riches; they commend voluntary poverty, lending without expectation of return, nonretaliation, rejoicing in the face of reproach, severance of family ties, a fearless and carefree attitude, confidence in God's care, a sense of vocation, discipleship without pretensions, and single-mindedness in the pursuit of God's reign.

The aphorisms of Q subvert the temperate, obedient worldview of the Hebrew Scriptures' collection, based on foresight and reaching toward order. They emphasize the importance of leaving room for self-questioning rather than providing sturdy moral grounds for judging others, a renunciation of established definitions of life as prosperity, large family, health, and good reputation, and the risk of confidence in the care of a loving God that elevates faith over foresight. The individual should give himself over to God's care, and out of that confidence, rather than out of anxiety, attend to matters that require foresight, common sense, and prudence. The anxious individual paradoxically defeats his own ends: "he loses what he most desires, life, by seeking it in an anxious, self-centered way. The way out of this predicament is to give up one's life in the sense perpetrated by traditional wisdom and to be committed to God's coming kingdom."[31]

The subversive proverbs attributed to Jesus in Q do not merely undercut expectations built up by traditional wisdom. While they reverse expectations, they also encourage hope. They build on the twin convictions that people are of great worth in God's eyes and that the possibility exists for change in individuals' situations. Asking leads to receiving. Giving up a current conception of life results in receiving a joyful new life. "The Kingdom demands all and at the same time gives all. The sharp demand for self-denial is joined in Q with a strong affirmation of the presence of salvation. This is evident, for example, in the beatitudes' promise of comfort and the theme of the eschatological banquet."[32]

Some of Jesus' Synoptic sayings mirror the wisdom of existing proverbs. Some examples are, that life should be lived one day at a time (Matt. 6:34), that the laborer deserves his food (Matt. 10:10/Luke 10:7), that one tends to see others' faults and ignore her own (Matt. 7:3, 4) that a tree is known by its fruit (Matt. 12:33/Luke 6:43), that one's life does not consist in the abundance of one's possessions (Matt. 12:15), and that a city on a hill cannot be hidden (Matt. 5:14).[33]

On the lips of the Synoptic Jesus, proverbs beyond Q, both quoted and coined, most often subvert rather than inculcate existing order. Jesus is depicted as discouraging a self-defeating care for maintaining ourselves in the world, which distracts us from reliance on God and seduces us into maintaining a status quo that values position and tradition over people. Life is to be found by giving up obsessive striving after self-order which manifests itself in the desire to build a good reputation with others based on public recognition of our generosity and piety (Matt. 6:1–6;16–18). Several aphorisms employ vivid scenes whose potential metaphorical applications challenge religious traditions. The reader is led to picture someone sewing unshrunken cloth on an old cloak, pouring new wine into old wineskins, a camel going through a needle's eye, hacking off or tearing out parts of one's body if they make one stumble. Other, literal aphorisms overturn traditional expectations about the pious life. Expectations of what is defiling are reversed, as is the significance of the Sabbath, and the definition of greatness.

The contours of subversive counter-order both within and beyond Q are revealed in what Jesus talked about, but also in those traditional wisdom themes conspicuous by their absence. Education, personal character and habits, friendship, family relationships, ethnic matters, politics, and prudence are all missing from the hundred or so proverbial sayings in the surviving Jesus traditions.[34]

Theological Norms

Q, as a sapiential sayings collection, makes a kerygmatic statement apart from the passion kerygma. The teacher, "Jesus, the Living One," is present in the words he has spoken. "Faith" is understood as belief in Jesus' words, a belief that makes what Jesus proclaimed present and real for the believer. The theological norm that motivated and pervades the collection is that the subversive sapiential teachings of Jesus are the loci for God's revelatory activity.[35]

The theological norm of Q2 has been shaped by the wider society's rejection of Q1's subversive way of life. Hence the shift from teaching to authority of teacher, as Jesus is identified as personified Wisdom's envoy and then as personified Wisdom herself, and in Q2, with the Son of Man figure of imminent apocalyptic judgment. These theological emphases that span Q1 and Q2 correspond to those explicitly stated in the proverbs of the Hebrew Scriptures' collection: that wisdom is a gift from God, in this case, in the form of the words and presence of Jesus; that acceptance of the teachings and the person of personified Wisdom (Jesus) is the beginning of wisdom, and finally, that wisdom is a body of instruction for the ordering (in this case, counter-ordering) of personal and social life, which one ignores or actively rejects at one's peril.

As the first century drew to a close, the *Logia sophōn* genre increasingly became associated with gnostic circles, and the gospel genre which culminated in a passion narrative gained ascendancy over it. The incorporation of Q's aphorisms into the gospel genre, while it obscured the collection's unique christological, theological focus, preserved sayings that otherwise might not have survived at all.

As in the case of proverbs inscribed in the book of Proverbs, while inscription preserves the proverbs and aphorisms of Q, it also removes them yet another step from their original situational context. Matthew at times places them in the specific conflictual contexts, implying that they are exclusively tied to these situations. Luke, by retaining them in large, unbroken segments, risks the misperception that these proverbs are universal truths, applicable for all situations.

In preaching Synoptic proverbs, their Q context needs to be acknowledged, but not allowed to become an interpretive cul-de-sac. Rather, it becomes a context within a context as the interpreter takes what he has learned about a saying from its Q context into its gospel context, considering the theological, historical-social, and literary norms of the gospel in which it is found. Consideration of the evangelist's unique audience, theological outlooks and motivations, and literary artistry come into play at this point.

This study has sought to revive the situationality of proverbs and aphorisms as partial truths which arise out of originative situations but which have the capacity to transcend them to speak to certain contemporary situations, but not to others. The hermeneutical openness of individual proverbs is best served when the preacher takes into account their Q and their gospel context, but neither limits their range to the specific situation in the gospel, nor universalizes them to blanket all human interactions.

Q's vision of Jesus' death is that it is the fate of all true envoys of Wisdom, a withdrawal of Wisdom until Jesus' return as the judging Son of Man. In between the believer is to have faith in Jesus the sage's words and Wisdom-in-person's presence offering guidance in present challenges. In preaching on proverbs from Q in the Synoptic Gospels, the preacher needs to hold these theological, christological insights of Q together with those of the narrative gospel genre's passion and resurrection. In this light, the cross represents the consequences of Jesus' living out his own subversive wisdom to the point of his own abuse and murder. The resurrection legitimizes Jesus' subversive teachings as in keeping with the Wisdom and reign of God. It is the assurance that Jesus' personal presence, Wisdom-in-Person, now pervades contemporary life.

Our preaching on proverbs is an ongoing process of actively attending to the wisdom sayings of Jesus the sage in the life of the community, and turning to his contemporary presence for the guidance we need in using these wisdom sayings. The cross witnesses to the high cost of adherence to Wisdom's subversive teachings, and the lengths to which Wisdom herself is continually willing to go to reconcile humans and divine. The resurrection ensures that it is the risen, living Christ who both guides preachers in contextualizing proverbs in contemporary life and empowers hearers in living by them.

The figure of personified Wisdom that arose in Proverbs remained an important symbol as Judaism developed in the Hellenistic world, focusing on her Greek name, Sophia. Both Sirach and the Wisdom of Solomon developed her portrait as acting at God's command, ordering the cosmos and revealing God to Israel.[36] Philo of Alexandria used Wisdom and Logos interchangeably as symbols of the working of God in the world, but insisting that the male Logos was superior to the female Wisdom, thus preparing the way for the substitution of Logos for Wisdom.[37]

Jesus himself may well have viewed himself as an envoy of Wisdom (Luke 7:33–35; Matt. 11:18–19). In the later layers of Q, as we have seen, Jesus is identified with Heavenly Wisdom herself. Paul proclaims

Christ crucified as "the power of God and the wisdom [Sophia] of God" (1 Cor. 1:24). Paul's use of Wisdom has an apocalyptic context; secret apocalyptic wisdom is not available in ordinary experience but is given in special revelation. As "the wisdom of God," Christ is the central, supremely important element in God's secret plan of salvation. In this same letter Paul began the tradition of attributing to Christ the cosmological role in creation that had been held by Wisdom (1 Cor. 8:6).[38]

Most influential of all for later Christian traditions, the prologue of the Gospel of John uses the language of Wisdom to describe the Word (Logos). Everything John says of the Logos could be said of Wisdom except for the identification of the Logos as God. The substitution of the masculine "Logos" for the feminine "Wisdom" (Sophia) is a choice that foreshadowed the later neglect of Wisdom in the West.

Most early church writers followed Philo's lead and identified Wisdom with the Logos, and thus, in light of the Fourth Gospel, with the divine in Jesus Christ. Others, like Irenaeus of Lyons, identified her with the third person of the Trinity (954). The affirmation of Sophia of Prov. 8:22–31 as fully divine and consubstantial with the Father was crucial for Athanasius's claim that Jesus was begotten by God and not a creature who had a beginning in time.[39]

So complete has been Wisdom's replacement by the Logos in later Western Christology that the revival of Wisdom language by feminists continues to churn up tidal waves of controversy. The reluctance on the part of many to consider recovering Wisdom as a metaphor for divine activity springs from the fear that she will be absolutized in the same way that the metaphor of God the Father has been. Because male metaphors have dominated the tradition for so long, Christians need to recover their heritage of female metaphors like Wisdom to do justice to both the biblical witness and the experience of women today.[40] Preachers can only gain from Wisdom's rescue from the obscurity to which a patriarchal bias has consigned her for centuries in Western Christianity to take her place in the rich repertoire of metaphors for divine activity offered to us by the biblical witness.

Literary Norms

Clearly, the literary norms of Proverbs embodied the theological and historical-social meta-norm of order. Just as clearly, the aphorisms and proverbs of Qohelet embodied theological and historical-social norms that subverted its adequacy as an all-encompassing guide to life. The literary norms of the Synoptic aphorisms both dismantle the ordered world as Qohelet did and suggest behaviors that craft a counter-order. Proverbs is characterized by the pairing of discrete proverbs with the personification of Wisdom and the dynamic of hearers' being summoned into the presence of the Wisdom figure and then sent out into their particular situations equipped with her proverbs. This same dynamic characterizes the Q document with its identification of Jesus with Wisdom and its inclusion of subversive proverbs, which equip the hearer to begin to craft counter-order patterns of behavior in the varied circumstances of daily life.

While our focus is on proverbs as discrete texts, the preacher must consider the broader Synoptic context of individual proverbs, both of the aphoristic cluster in which they often occur and the even larger context of the theological and literary aims of the total gospel. The preacher considers these contextual concerns when researching the repertoire of the proverbial text: its theological, literary, and historical-social norms.

The proverbs attributed to Jesus in the Synoptic Gospels evince what William Beardslee calls a "distinctive intensification of proverbial wisdom," by means of paradox, reversal, and hyperbole.[41] Charles Carlston confirms that, while the Jesus tradition employs the traditional form of the proverb, it portrays Jesus' proverbial teaching as different from its precursors in the Hebrew Scriptures in its use of hyperbole, its paradoxical formulations, its extremism, its demand for bold action, and its eschatological conditioning.[42]

Equational Forms

We recall that in Proverbs, the primary form of proverbs of chapters 16—22 is synonymous parallelism, in which the second descriptive element (topic-comment unit) does not merely repeat, but strengthens and even extends the language and content of the first. Several Synoptic proverbs are characterized by synonymous parallelism:

> Prophets are not without honor except in their own country and in their own house. (Matt. 13:57 = Mark 6:4; note that Luke 4:24 and John 4:44 treat it as a folk saying)
>
> A disciple is not above the teacher, nor a slave above the master. (Matt. 10:24; Luke 6:40a; John 13:16; 15:20)
>
> Nothing is covered up that will not be uncovered, and

nothing secret that will not become known. (Matt.
10:26 = Mark 4:22; Luke 8:17; 12:2, 3)

In Proverbs, one prominent equational form was similitudes or
comparative proverbs, which make analogies between the natural
realm and the human realm. In the Synoptic sayings, these are expressed as rhetorical questions, which beg a negative answer, implying that what is impossible in the natural realm by analogy is foolish
in the human realm. Aspects of the natural realm are called upon to
undercut current human practices rather than to substantiate them.
Thus rather than equational proverbs, they become more oppositional, in light of natural self-evidence, exposing human absurdity.[43]

"Are grapes gathered from thorns, or figs from thistles?" (Matt.
7:16 = Luke 6:44). "Is a lamp brought in to be put under the bushel
basket, or under the bed, and not on the lampstand?" (Mark 4:21 =
Matt. 5:15; Luke 11:33). "Salt is good; but if salt has lost its saltiness,
how can you season it?" (Mark 9:50 = Matt. 5:13 = Luke 14:34).[44]

Sometimes they are expressed in statement form: "No one sews a
piece of unshrunk cloth on an old cloak, for the patch pulls away from
the cloak and a worse tear is made" (Matt. 9:16; Luke 5:36). "Neither is new wine put into old wineskins; otherwise, the skins burst,
and the wine is spilled, and the skins are destroyed"(Matt. 9:17).
"Foxes have holes, and birds of the air have nests; but the Son of Man
has nowhere to lay his head" (Luke 9:58).

Oppositional Forms

Moving beyond comparison and analogy one comes to "better than"
sayings that make value judgments between two sharply drawn alternatives. "It is better for you to enter life maimed than to have two
hands and to go to hell"(Mark 9:43). "It is better for you to enter life
lame than to have two feet and to be thrown into hell"(9:45). "It is
better for you to enter the kingdom of God with one eye than to have
two eyes and to be thrown into hell" (Mark 9:47/Matt. 5:29–30;
18:8–9). A "better than" saying may reside behind Mark 9:42 (=
Luke 17:1–2/Matt. 18:6). These Synoptic "better than" sayings ac-
centuate the undesirability of what is preferred in and of itself, until
viewed in light of its alternative. What the synoptic saying says is better is horrible, but the alternative is even more horrible. In the case
of the Proverbs' "better thans," the preferred is not painted with such
dramatic horror; it is merely undesirable (Prov. 16:8; 17:1; 27:5).

Just as antithetical parallelism occurs in Proverbs, primarily the proverbs in chapters 10—15, so it manifests itself as the form of some of the sayings attributed to Jesus.

> Foxes have holes, and birds of the air have nests; but the Son of Man has nowhere to lay his head. (Matt. 8:20 = Luke 9:58)

> The good person brings good things out of a good treasure, and the evil person brings evil things out of an evil treasure. (Matt. 12:35 = Luke 6:45)

> Many are called, but few are chosen. (Matt. 22:14)

> Those who are well have no need of a physician, but those who are sick. (Mark 2:17 = Matt. 9:12 = Luke 5:31)

> The spirit indeed is willing, but the flesh is weak. (Mark 14:38 = Matt. 26:41)[45]

Paradoxical Proverbs

More pronounced than antithetical parallelism in the Synoptic sayings is a type of literal proverb called paradoxical proverbs. Such paradoxical heightening of tensions is rare in Proverbs, far more common in Qohelet and in the Synoptic Gospels. Robert Tannehill calls these paradoxical proverbs "antithetical aphorisms."[46] Conventional wisdom predictably pairs good behavior with good results and foolish behavior with ruinous results. Jesus' proverbs at times paradoxically pair what is viewed as good by conventional wisdom with ruinous results and what is viewed as negative by conventional wisdom with positive results.

For example,

> There is nothing outside a person that by going in can defile, but the things that come out are what defile. (Mark 7:15 = Matt. 15:11)

> Whoever wants to be first must be last of all and servant of all. (Mark 9:35 = Matt. 20:26–27 = Luke 22:26)

> For those who want to save their life will lose it, and those who lose their life for my sake, and for the sake of the gospel, will save it. (Mark 8:35 = Luke 9: 24; 17:33 = Matt. 10:39)

> All who exalt themselves will be humbled, and all who humble themselves will be exalted. (Matt. 23:12 = Luke 14:11)[47]

> To those who have, more will be given, and they will have an abundance; but from those who have nothing, even what they have will be taken away. (Matt. 13:12 = 25:29 = Luke 19:26)

> Many who are first will be last, and the last will be first. (Matt. 19:30 = Matt. 20:16 = Luke 13:30)

Neither reason nor common sense is appealed to. These paradoxes combine a sharp attack on prevailing perspectives and a lack of concern for practicalities or compromise. They disorient us into living with disorder as a counter-order arrives. By their tension of opposites, they undercut and overturn normative wisdom's definitions of wisdom and folly and subvert the quest for the orderly life (88f.).

They are also capable of suggesting patterns of positive subversive behavior in contemporary situations. These performative qualities of the antithetical aphorisms or paradoxical proverbs are shared by what Tannehill calls "focal instances."[48] "It is easier for a camel to go through the eye of a needle than for someone who is rich to enter the kingdom of God" (Matt. 19:24 = Mark 10:25 = Luke 18:25). "Let the dead bury their own dead"(Matt. 8:22 = Luke 9:60). "If anyone strikes you on the right cheek, turn the other also; and if anyone wants to sue you and take your coat, give your cloak as well; and if anyone forces you to go one mile, go also the second mile" (Matt. 5:39–41).

These sayings picture a specific scene and make a statement or command relative to that scene. They are characterized by specificity, and they either imply an exaggerated judgment or make an extreme, outright demand (hyperbole). By their hyperbole and specificity, they transcend the particular scene they depict and make themselves available as proverbs, which seek to be apt fits with situations that fall within the broader fields of experience to which they point—retaliation, forgiveness, private charity and public opinion, inward motives and outward acts, family ties and the kingdom's call. They do not pretend to be legal rules, meant to be enforced as general regulations at their literal level of meaning. They function like proverbs, seeking to find an apt fit with situations of daily life, in which they defamiliarize us to our habitual, deeply ingrained patterns of thinking and behavior.[49] The purpose of this rhetorical strategy is to contrast the advocated teaching with conventional human behavior, thereby inducing a new way of looking at a whole field of behavior.

Frank Kermode has perceptively called this strategy of hyperbole a "rhetoric of excess." It is especially prominent in the Sermon on the Mount in a series of contrasts between the old Torah and the new commandments of the messianic teacher. The "rhetoric of excess" strongly implies the assumption that the authority of the individual teacher supersedes the Pharisaic-rabbinic tradition of the fathers, the authority of the sages of the past who had transmitted the oral revelation given at Sinai (*Aboth* 1:1). For Matthew, Jesus is the one whose teachings embody the new order of God for the messianic community his gospel addresses.[50]

Table 6.2
Synoptic Proverbs

Matthew's Gospel

4:4	6:22	8:20, 22	10:26b	12:34b	15:27	20:16
5:3–11	6:24	9:12	10:37–41	12:50	16:24–26	20:26–27
5:13b	6:25b	9:13a	11:19b	13:12	17:20	22:14
5:14b	6:26b–27	9:15	11:30	13:57	18:8, 9	22:21
5:15	6:34b	9:16	12:7	15:11	18:18–20	23:12
5:29–30	7:2–5	9:17	12:25	15:13	19:6b	24:28
5:39b–41	7:8	9:37	12:29	15:14	19:24	24:43
5:46, 47	7:16b	10:10b	12:30	15:26	19:30	26:41b
6:21	7:18	10:24	12:32–33			26:52b

Mark's Gospel

2:17	2:28	4:22	7:27	9:40	10:25
2:19	3:24	4:24	7:28	9:43	10:31
2:21	3:25	4:25	8:35	9:45	10:43–44
2:22	3:27	6:4	8:36	10:9	12:17
2:27	4:21	7:15	9:35	10:15	

Luke's Gospel

4:4	6:33–34	8:18	10:7b	12:15	14:34	18:27
4:24	6:38c	9:24	11:10	12:24	16:10	19:26
5:31	6:39–45b	9:25	11:17	12:34	16:13	20:18
5:36–38	6:49	9:48	11:23	12:39	16:15b	20:25
5:39	7:35	9:58	11:33	12:48b	17:33	22:26
6:20–22	7:47	9:60	11:34	13:30	17:37	
6:23–26	8:16	9:62	12:2	14:11	18:14	
6:29	8:17	10:2	12:3	14:28	18:25	

Impossible Questions

One of the forms that was relatively scarce in Proverbs compared to Job, Qohelet, and the Synoptic sayings is the impossible question, which points to the limits of human knowledge and the inscrutability of God.

This form characterizes several of the Synoptic sayings, where it functions to highlight the opposition between current human practices and God's present and coming reign.

> If you love those who love you, what reward do you have? (Matt. 5:46
>   = Luke 6:32)
> If you do good to those who do good to you, what credit is that to
>   you?" (Luke 6:33)
> If you lend to those from whom you hope to receive, what credit is
>   that to you?" (Luke 6:34)
> And if you greet only your brothers and sisters, what more are you do-
>   ing than others?" (Matt. 5:47)
> "Why do you see the speck in your neighbor's eye, but do not notice
>   the log in your own eye?" (Matt. 7:3 = Luke 6:41)
> For what will it profit them to gain the whole world and forfeit their
>   life?" (Mark 8:36 = Matt. 16:26 = Luke 9:25)
> Salt is good; but if the salt has lost its saltiness, how can you season it?"
>   (Mark 9:50;Matt. 5:13; Luke 14:34)
> And can any of you by worrying add a single hour to your span of
>   life?" (Matt. 6:27 = Luke 12:25).

In the case of Jesus' proverbs, the narrator is not the common, order-inculcating wisdom of the community, but the fresh, order-subverting wisdom of an individual. Jesus' sayings become the theme by which a proverb reader can look out over the horizon of her life. They cause us to question habitual ways of defining the good life, urgent priorities, and appropriate behaviors, and to consider and act on subversive alternatives in specific situations (see table 6.2).[51]

7

No Fear, Just Do It: Contemporary Proverbs

ontemporary proverbs come from a variety of sources, re-flecting the multiculturalism that has always been operative in America. Folk sources in the United States include not only the Anglo-Celtic, but also, among others, African-American, native American, Hispanic, Latino, Mexican-American, Asian-American, Puerto Rican, French, Cajun, Creole, German-American, Polish-American, Scandinavian, Italian, and Jewish.[1]

Of course in contemporary American life, no collected body of proverbs serves as a uniformly agreed-on "normative wisdom." Certain values of hard work, moderation, and foresight pervade proverbs that come from a variety of ethnic/cultural groups and thereby deserve the label "traditional." An exhaustive discussion of proverbs from every ethnic and cultural group in contemporary American life is beyond the scope of this chapter. It is hoped that the reader will be inspired to explore that body of wisdom, both ordering and subverting, which is operative in his congregational context.

CONTEMPORARY PROVERBS THAT CREATE ORDER

Poor Richard's Proverbs

An excellent place to start in discussing contemporary American proverbs of order is with the wisdom sayings of Benjamin Franklin's *Poor Richard's Almanac,* brief educational booklets published annually from 1733 to 1758 under the name of Richard Saunders. They embody a pragmatic worldview that continues to influence contemporary American wisdom. Franklin coined only about 5 percent of the proverbs, borrowing the rest from other sources, often rephrasing them to be more memorable. Next to the Bible the almanacs were probably the most frequent reading material in the colonies. For coping with the circumstances of daily life, the almanacs took on the role of secular Bible. "If the stout preachers of the pulpit quoted Solomon's Biblical proverbs, the common citizens would cite the wisdom of Poor Richard."[2]

The best seller of all his almanacs, entitled "The Way to Wealth," was a masterful treatise advocating industry as the way to prosperity. A smattering of its contents reveals a surface similarity with many of the sayings in Proverbs. "He that goes a-borrowing goes a-sorrowing." "Diligence is the mother of good luck." "Experience keeps a dear school, but fools will learn in no other, and scarce in that." "Laziness travels so slowly that poverty soon overtakes it." "Many estates are spent in the getting, since women for tea forsook spinning and knitting, and men for punch forsook hewing and splitting." "Time-enough always proves little enough." "The sleeping fox catches no poultry." "Early to bed, early to rise, makes a man healthy, wealthy, and wise"(adapted from a fifteenth-century English proverb) (Mieder, 131–33).

Clearly the historical-social norm of these sayings is that industry and moderation lead to life defined in material terms. The theological norms of Poor Richard's proverbs are explicitly stated in several sayings. "In the affairs of this world, men are saved, not by faith, but by the want of it." "He that lives upon hopes will die fasting." "God helps them that help themselves." "God gives all things to industry."

Many American proverbs continue to conform to the contours of Poor Richard's wisdom of order. The cultural axioms they convey are, like his, conducive to capitalistic accomplishment. Four common cultural axioms are visual empiricism, pluralism, the notion that everything can be measured in terms of its monetary worth, and the conviction of unlimited good and unfettered progress. Visual empiricism is conveyed by such sayings as "Seeing is believing," "A picture is worth a thousand words," and "What you see is what you get." Pluralism is the theme of "Different strokes for different folks" and "Whatever turns you on." Money as the measure of all things expresses itself through "Money talks," "Money makes the world go around," "You get what you pay for," "Time is money," and "Every-one has his price." "Unlimited good and unfettered progress are en-capsulated in "There's more where that came from," "The sky's the limit," and "Records were made to be broken."[3]

Several uniquely American proverbs coined in this century both reflect and shape this milieu. They include "The grass is always greener on the other side of the fence," what Wolfgang Mieder calls "An American proverb of discontent"; "A picture is worth a thousand words," which reflects the visual preoccupation of American culture; and a proverb that originated in African-American communities of the late 1940s in the southern United States and reflects the pluralism characteristic of American life: "Different strokes for different folks."[4]

Proverbial Promotions

A number of sayings coined by individuals have been promoted to proverbial status in the United States in this century. Sayings "make it" when they resonate with an underlying theme or cultural axiom of a society, so they are a window onto aspects of its worldview. Those quotable quotes which have become proverbs cluster around several cultural axioms. Again, by no coincidence, they are proverbs of which Poor Richard would be proud!

The importance of perseverance is expressed in several now proverbial twentieth-century sayings. "When the going gets tough, the tough get going" is attributed to President Kennedy's father, Joseph P. Kennedy, out of the context of the Boston-Irish political jungle. "Never say die!" was a line from a novel by Charles Dickens. President Harry Truman first said, "If you can't stand the heat, get out of the kitchen." "We shall not be moved" originated from an African-American spiritual echoing a number of psalms. It was later taken up as a song of the civil rights and labor movements of the 1960s. "Be-cause it's there" was spoken by mountaineer George Leigh Mallory in 1923 when someone asked him why he wanted to scale Mount Everest. He disappeared one year later in his final attempt.

"The buck stops here," an affirmation of personal responsibility, was coined by Harry Truman, deriving from a poker player's expres-sion referring to a marker that can be passed on by someone who doesn't wish to deal. When President Nixon published his memoirs (1978), people opposed to its sale went around wearing buttons that said, "The book stops here." "There is no such thing as a free lunch" is a saying from the 1840s that refers to the thirst-arousing snacks (pretzels) on the counters of saloon bars. Economist Milton Friedman revived it in the 1970s. Two related sayings are "There's no getting something for nothing," and the bargain hunter's nemesis: "You get what you pay for."[5]

"Can Do" Proverbs

A number of contemporary motivational proverbs have their home in the business and sports worlds, which I call the "can-do collection." They define life as the attainment of personal goals, whether in sports, business, or some other arena, with its attendant satisfaction. One attains life by discipline and positive attitude. These sayings emphasize leadership, risk taking, commitment, and enthusiasm, all excellent qualities. And they promote them in portable, memorable form. So far, so good.

The problem arises when the perpetrators of these proverbs forget the proverb's character as partial generalization, and promote them as relevant to all of life. Then these "can-do" proverbs make promises that are quickly ground underfoot by life. For they promise an unbreakable link between positive attitudes and behaviors and positive outcomes, without regard for the limitations of individual capabilities or circumstances or systemic injustices. They promise that if one takes initiative, sets goals, is willing to work up a sweat, possesses a can-do approach, is attentive to detail in the pursuit of excellence, and perseveres, one will attain life. They define life in largely individualistic terms, and exalt a positive attitude as the omnipotent force in the cosmos. Some of these sayings are familiar favorites of American cultural wisdom, some are the invention of famous individuals, and still others are newly minted by companies that produce motivational products for businesses and individuals.

If Ben Franklin were alive today, he would no doubt be avidly culling sayings for his annual almanacs from all these sources. He would be sitting at his computer, thumbing through the latest Successories catalog, a copy of *See You at the Top,* by Zig Ziglar, on his desk, sipping coffee from his "No Goals, No Glory" mug. For this contemporary "can-do" collection is right up his alley.

The importance of attitude is thematic in these contemporary proverbs. "If it's going to be, it's up to me" (Robert H. Schuller). "Opportunities are disguised by hard work, so most people don't recognize them." "Attitudes are contagious. Is yours worth catching?" "Attitude is everything." "A positive attitude creates positive results." "The pleasure you get from your life is equal to the attitude you put into it." "I can complain because rosebushes have thorns or rejoice because the thornbush has a rose." "The only limits are those of vision." A positive attitude toward adversity is advocated by several of these proverbs. "Don't fear the winds of adversity. A kite rises against the wind, not with it." "In the middle of every difficulty lies an opportunity." "Anyone can hold the helm when the sea is calm." "Keep your face to the sunshine and you cannot see the shadows."

Perseverance is a theme of many of these sayings. "Inch by inch, life's a cinch. Yard by yard, life is hard"(Robert H. Schuller). "No goals, no glory." "Never, never quit." "The race is not always to the swift, but to those who keep on running." "Persistence prevails when all else fails."

A number of sayings come from the arena of sports and the pursuit of physical excellence. "The spirit to win and the will to excel is always measured one stroke at a time" (caption to a picture of a swimmer). "A champion is someone who gets up even when they can't"(caption to a picture of a runner getting up off the track). "To be a winner, all you need to give is all you have."

Several "success" proverbs talk about teamwork, but the purpose of teamwork is to provide a context in which individual goals can be better accomplished. "Together everyone achieves more." "Teamwork means less me and more we." "Teamwork is the fuel that allows common people to attain uncommon results."

Some of these proverbs subvert an exclusive focus on individual success by alluding to the existence of a higher goal. These subversive sayings are simply not plentiful enough to stage a successful coup against the "can-do," "get out on the field and win" sayings. Nor are they just outnumbered; they are contradicted and overpowered by the peppy "can-dos." In comparison, these softer, gentler sayings seem to range from unbelievable, "Pride inspires us, not to get ahead of others, but to get ahead of ourselves," to patronizing, "No exercise is better for the heart than reaching out and lifting people up," to wishful thinking, "Success is a journey, not a destination," to comically vague, "In the race to be better or best, do not miss the joy of being." The joy of being what? God forbid that these sweet, vague sayings should ever be let loose in the boardroom or, worse yet, the locker room. They would quickly be trampled to death by the can-dos in their hustle to get out on the field.

"No Fear" Proverbs

An even more aggressive group of contemporary proverbial sayings is waiting out on the playing field. They are the can-do proverbs on steroids. They appear on the T-shirts marketed by the "No Fear: Dangerous Sports Gear" Company through sporting goods and de-partment stores. Flipping through the T-shirts on the rack, at first one thinks they are offering helpful advice to the young and athletic about looking fear in the eyes, taking risks, making a big effort, and earnestly desiring to reach one's goal. "Fear: just another four-letter word." "Wherever the fear may be, look it in the eyes." "Life is a contact sport." "Heaven is living in your hopes. Hell is living in your fears." "Everybody who lives dies. But not everybody who dies has lived." "It's not how good you are, it's how bad you want it." "It's not how big you are. It's how big you play."

Some are worth a chuckle. "I've never lost. I've just been a little behind when time ran out." "Who says Sunday is a day of rest?" (cap-tion to a picture of football players). "For every battle there's a price. Now pick up your teeth and go home."

But the chuckle fades as one continues flipping through the shirts on the rack, reading saying after saying. "No chickens, no wimps, no losers." "It must be hard living without a spine." "No crybabies. Not so much as a whimper." "If you don't want to win no one will stop you." "I don't come here to play, I come here to win." "Winners do what losers didn't." "If it were just about attitude, everyone would have it."

"Jump from the cliff to fly, not to fall." "Know your limits, then break 'em." "Living with boundaries is not living." "Why run when you can fly?" "Live free or die." "Where I come from there is no next time, there is no second chance, there is no time out."

"Pain is just part of the game." "Pain is temporary. Glory is for-ever." "I feel a bruise on your horizon." And the worst of the bunch, while not exactly proverbial, tells us worlds about all the others that are. "I am a predator. I smell your fear. I can sense your fright. I will prey on you. Because I can."

The no-fear sayings' expansion of the competitive attitude appro-priate to field and rink to encompass all the territories of one's life makes them "dangerous sports gear" in a moral sense. They express a blanket condemnation of limits and boundaries, an uncritically positive evaluation of pain and risk, a worship of winning, and a hostile attitude toward weakness of any kind. One can think of a few situations in which these sayings might be quoted as words of encouragement to excel, but lots more where they could be quoted to make other people feel bad about themselves, their performance, and their lives in general. Of course, on the no-fear field of life, since those people are losers anyway, it doesn't really matter how they feel. What matters is that they pick up their teeth and make their way to the sidelines, to take their proper place as spectators to the game of life, which can only be played by the winners, the young, the healthy, the aggressive.

Can-do proverbs of the less ominous Successories variety, when divorced from materialistic goals and attached to laudable ones, can be invaluable tools in building group identity and motivation. A body of proverbs used in many drug and alcohol abuse recovery programs conveys the message that life means an end to substance dependence to be gained by dependence on one's own will and the support of the therapeutic group. Proverbs are used to inculcate the group's rules in the new member of the group and to warn of difficult times to come. "No rewards for bad behavior," "No pain, no gain," "When the going gets tough, the tough get going," and "You alone can do it, but you cannot do it alone." Once in the group, proverbs are used to strengthen the member's commitment to the group and its values. "Hang tough." After graduation, proverbs serve as a powerful reminder when one is confronted with situations in which one is tempted to deviate from the treatment program. "Only the strong survive."[6]

The can-do sayings, with their emphasis on the importance of perseverance and an upbeat attitude even in the midst of adversity, contain a crucial grain of truth. Certainly Christians accomplish more with less whining, more creative imagining of the redemptive possibilities that lie within tragedies, and greater commitment to the long haul. By themselves our can-do secular proverbs show an aversion to facing the existence of outward tragedies and inward turmoils deeper than the power of human attitude to overcome. If Christian preachers are going to use them to motivate people to hold onto their faith and persevere in the face of difficulties, these proverbs must be put into a theological context where attitude is undergirded by faith, where perseverance is toward godly goals, and where adversities are not always stepping-stones to greater career advancement, but may be unspeakable tragedies which only God can give the strength to survive, or setbacks one might take on willingly in an overweening desire to help another.

Religious "Self-Help" Proverbs

The secular "can-do" wisdom of the Successories variety appears with a religious veneer in the contemporary genre of inspirational literature, defined as "self-help books with religious overtones which offer advice on how to raise one's self image and succeed in worldly affairs."[7] The authors of this literature use existing sayings and coin new ones to convey a wisdom of order whose dominant definition of life is material success. Present, but outnumbered and outmaneuvered, are sayings that define life as altruism. In attempting to combine these two definitions of life the authors are reflecting the uneasy alliance they share in the American Dream.

That uneasy alliance is not as offensive in sayings that are avowedly secular. But religious self-help literature seeks to legitimize materialism by appealing to religious traditions, oftentimes to biblical proverbial sayings. Preachers need to be familiar enough with the biblical proverbial heritage to rescue it from this hostage situation.

Inspirational literature's proverbs define wisdom as the pursuit and attainment of individual material success, without regard for personal or circumstantial limits, implying that such success is a sign of God's favor. To promote this definition of wisdom they quote and coin proverbs that sanction wealth, individualism, and achievement.

They even quote biblical proverbs in a selective and often distorted way, in an attempt to prove that the Bible views the pursuit of wealth in an uncritically positive way. Schuller uses Jesus' words, "You have not because you ask not" to encourage his readers to borrow money. Ziglar (6–10) quotes Psalm 1:3 and Malachi 3:10 to prove "that money is scripturally okay." The Bible is used as a pawn in the attempt to dissolve the tension between worldly success and altruism for their readers (Arthurs, 8).

The good news these writers preach through their proverbs is the efficacy of individual effort over environment, of hard work over circumstances. Positive outlook and effort are the path to attaining life defined as material success. Get worked up about your job and you will work your job up (Peale, 6). Will you stare up the steps or step up the stairs? (Ziglar, 6). Attitude is more important than aptitude (Ziglar,

6). "Most of the shadows of this life are caused by standing in our own sunshine"(Peale quoting Ralph Waldo Emerson, 8). Carnegie quotes Shakespeare's "Thinking makes it so," to buttress the point that individual will, not circumstances, gives the orders to destiny. These authors verbalize their audience's hope that worldly success is the inevitable result of self-assertion (Arthurs, 8).

Some of the proverbs quoted in this "can-do" inspirational literature embody the norm that success in life cannot be reduced to material prosperity alone, but includes concern for the welfare of others, charity, and service. Schuller quotes Shakespeare: "To err is human, to forgive divine." Carnegie uses Jesus' proverb "Judge not that ye be not judged" to argue for the value of tolerance. Charity and service are advocated in proverbs quoted by Schuller, such as "Bloom where you're planted" and "Rats flee a sinking ship"; and Ziglar: "Duty makes us do things well, but love makes us do them beautifully" (9, 10).

A couple of proverbs subvert the equation of success with life. "Not to win is not a sin" (Schuller). "Real failure is to fail as a person" (Schuller). Since the reader has already gotten the message that success as a person means attaining material prosperity, this is cold comfort for those who continue to be fiscally challenged. "Winning is not everything, but the effort to win is" (Ziglar). These nods to a more profound view of life are neither frequent nor enthusiastic enough to form a counter-order of subversive wisdom, but are overcome by the ethos of self-interest that equates life with personal success defined in largely material terms.

The proverbs of contemporary inspirational literature present a theologically limited view of wisdom, God, and Jesus. Wisdom becomes the pursuit of material success, God becomes its legitimizer, and Jesus becomes a motivational speaker. Missing from the can-do preacher's theological repertoire is the Proverbs' insistence that fearing the Lord is the beginning of wisdom and that the best laid human plans must humble themselves before the unpredictability of life and the sovereignty of God. Qohelet's sensitivity to the sufferings of those for whom the old equation of good life with good fortune doesn't hold does not compute with this contemporary wisdom of order. Jesus' insistence that "many who are first will be last, and the last will be first" (Mark 10:31 and parallels) subverts it to its very foundations.

A powerful order-inculcating function of proverbs is their use in advertising, where proverbs' traditionality legitimizes various products and indoctrinates the populace into their proper identity as "consumers." Sometimes the proverb is left intact. For example, a Burlington, Vermont, savings bank uses not just one but three proverbs as headlines: "The early bird gets the worm," "A stitch in time saves nine," and "A penny saved is a penny earned."[8] Other times the proverb is changed to reflect the specific product being pitched. "Thirst come, thirst served" (Coca-Cola Company, 1932) (Mieder and Mieder, 313). An ad campaign in the 1970s for Jones New York clothing depicted women in fashionable clothing with the caption, "Jones New York: No wonder everyone is trying to keep up with us." Whether used intact, in part, or parodied, proverbs' aura of traditional authority is being exploited to sell a product. In some cases companies aspire to that traditionality by coining proverblike slogans such as, for example, Nike's "Just Do It!" and Saab's "Find Your Own Road."

Proverbial slogans in advertising mirror the cultural axioms of American culture. Proverbs both reflect and then shape the worldviews of a people. Unfortunately, the advertising industry has mastered this insight far more effectively than Christian preachers. When a preacher knows her own biblical proverbial heritage and is attuned to how proverbs are in constant use in her culture, she is equipped to offer the dehumanized consumers in the pews an alternative identity, worldview, and way of life.

Traditional African-American Proverbs

African-American proverbs from the era of slavery sound many themes familiar to us from Proverbs and contemporary wisdom of order. But missing from them is the linkage of order with material prosperity. Rather, the focus is on survival and the habits of life, speech, and thought most conducive to it. The importance of hard work is expressed by such sayings as "The good farmer keeps acquainted with the daybreak," "You can't hurry up good times by waiting for them," and "Lazy folks' stomachs don't get tired." "A sleepy fisherman totes a light load home." "Ain't nothin to it but to do it." The dangers of excess is the theme of "Liquor talks mighty loud when it gets loose from the jug." Other proverbs sound the theme that hard work is better than pipe dreams. "You can't buy corn with the bag of gold at the end of the rainbow." "Countin' the stars doesn't help the meal-box." Advice not to boast of prospects that are not yet realities comes through in "Don't sell the bearskin till you done caught the bear,"

"Get the candles lighted before you blow out the match," and "You can't pick your fish before you catch them."

Several proverbs that originated in African-American contexts have become household sayings today. They sound themes of the tie between act and consequence, the importance of survival in a hostile environment, and the superiority of action to talk. "What goes around comes around." "Do unto others, before they do unto you." "Give some people an inch and they think they're a ruler." "Life isn't a bowl of cherries." "It takes one to know one." "You have to pay to play." "Put up or shut up." And "Different strokes for different folks" (Mieder, *American Proverbs*, 126).

Proverbs' order-inculcating dynamic can be associated with a laudable goal, such as freeing oneself from drug dependency, or the survival of a community in hostile conditions. It can also be associated with materialism where it can become a competitive and individualistic rhetorical force. The most sinister order-inculcating social function of proverbs is in oppressing groups that do not have power in a society.

Oppressive Proverbs

Misogynist proverbs are rampant in many cultures, so much so that in many proverb collections almost every proverb that touches on women contains a severe negation of the value of women in society. "A woman is only a woman, but a good cigar is a smoke."[9] "A woman is the weaker vessel." "A woman's answer is never to seek." "A woman's tongue wags like a lamb's tail." "All women may be won." "Women are as wavering as the wind." "Women naturally deceive, weep, and spin." "Women in state affairs are like monkeys in glass houses." And "Women are necessary evils."[10] A strong strain of anti-women proverbs is to be found in Proverbs itself (19:13; 27:15).

The downside of the wisdom of order, its tendency to dominate less powerful social groups, is revealed in some ugly frontier proverbs: "The only good Indian is a dead Indian," and "Indians will be Indians," a variation of the English proverb "Boys will be boys" from the sixteenth century. Missionaries are probably responsible for the following proverbs ascribed to the Winnebago Indians of Wisconsin, but in which are seen the need for the settlers to impose their proverbial and biblical wisdom on the populations they encountered: "It is not good to gamble." "Be on friendly terms with everyone, and everyone will love you." "Marry only one person at a time." "All persons dislike a borrower." "No one mourns the thriftless." "A man must make his own arrows."

Just as proverbs have been used to keep women in their place, so they have been used to reinforce white domination of blacks in this country. An African-American saying based on myriad observations of unfair treatment advises that "If you're black, get back; if you're white, you're right." These African-American sages saw all too clearly that, in the eyes of dominant wisdom, "Two blacks will never make a white," and "If you're white, you're all right; if you're brown, stick around; but if you're black, get back."[11] These self-deprecating proverbs show how a dominated group tends to internalize its low esteem in the eyes of a dominant group. They can be subverted by positive-identity-forming proverbs coined by a suppressed group.

CONTEMPORARY PROVERBS
THAT SUBVERT ORDER

Groups on the fringes, those not benefiting from the dominant social order, have sages of their own, often anonymous, who coin proverbs that challenge majority values. Not everybody in America, historically or today, has believed in the values of visual empiricism, pluralism, money as the measure of all things, and unlimited supply of goods as necessarily good. The order of visual empiricism is subverted by a powerful tradition of proverbs that insist that seeing may not be a reliable guide to accurate believing because realities to be reckoned with lie beneath the surface of life. "Appearances are deceiving." "You can't judge a book by its cover." "You can't judge a car by its paint job." From the slave quarters comes the reminder that "Can't tell much about a chicken pie till you get through the crust." "The wheat crop can't fool you when it comes to the thrashing" (*American Proverbs*, 121–22).

Money as the measure of all things is subverted by "Money can't buy happiness," "Money is the root of all evil" (a twisting of 1 Tim. 6:10, which actually says, "The love of money is a root of all kinds of evil"), and "Love makes the world go around."

The existence of unlimited good is challenged by "Waste not, want not," and "More than enough is more than enough wasted."

Proverbs Expressing Life's Downside

We have examined several "proverbial promotions": sayings that have arisen from specific twentieth-century contexts to the status of household saying. Many of them echo the sanguine sentiments of the "can do" family of sayings. Others boldly overlook the positive and the possibilities to bring to our attention the downside of life. The difficulty of life is acknowledged in several sayings: "Life wasn't meant to be easy" is a proverbial saying drawn from a line in George Bernard Shaw. Closely related is the saying "I never promised you a rose garden," from the title of a 1964 best-selling novel by Joanne Greenberg and a song inspired by it in 1971. "It never rains but it pours," which originated in a 1911 Morton salt ad, laments the fact that misfortunes never come singly. "You can run but you can't hide," is from boxer Joe Louis referring to Billy Conn, his opponent in a world heavyweight championship fight in June 1946. Billy was a fast mover, but Louis won the fight on a knockout. "This, too, shall pass away" is a quote from Nathaniel Hawthorne's *The Marble Faun;* it was more recently used as a song title by George Harrison, "All Things Must Pass" (1970), and Chuck Berry "Pass Away" (1979).

Pessimistic observations about human relations are the theme of several other sayings. For example, "Laugh and the world laughs with you. Weep and you weep alone" is a cynical proverb that comes from a poem by Ella Wheeler Wilcox (1855–1919) titled, appropriately, "Solitude." "I can look after my enemies, but God protect me from my friends" and "With friends like that who needs enemies?" are two sayings with obvious similarities. Novelist Charlotte Brontë used the latter in lamenting a patronizing review of one of her books.

The unpredictability of life is expressed by several sayings. "That's the way the cookie crumbles" is an anonymous phrase from the 1950s. "It seemed like a good idea at the time" is a proverbial saying used as a limp excuse when something has gone awry. It caught on in the 1950s. "Anything can happen and probably will" was a line from a radio program that ran from 1948 to 1959.[12]

Proverbs Parodying Traditional Values

One dynamic by which proverbs show their subversive potential is in proverb parodies, variations on existing proverbs that change their meaning. This is the dynamic Qohelet uses when he parodies the "better than" form: "Better the day of death than the day of birth." Similarly, contemporary proverb parodies challenge traditional values of morality and politics. Graffiti authors often choose to express themselves in proverb parodies, because, like the act of illegally scrawling on a bathroom or subway wall, they challenge authority. During the 1960s and 1970s proverb parodies were a genre of choice among countercultural youth who termed themselves in graffiti "the people our parents warned us about." In their graffiti, they subverted traditional proverbs in praise of sexual nonconformity and drug taking. "A friend with a weed is a friend indeed." "The grass is always greener on the other side of the border." "Never pull off tomorrow what you can pull off today." "Chastity is its own punishment." "Blessed are the pure, for they shall inhibit the earth." "A pill a day keeps the stork away." "A pill in time saves nine months." "Children should be seen and not had."

Other proverb parodies in graffiti express the social views of those who scrawl them. "No nukes is good nukes." "Dow shalt not kill." "Blood is thicker than oil." "Ronald Reagan is his own reward"(1967 when Reagan was governor of California).[13]

T-shirt quotations of the past couple of decades offer subversive commentary on traditional values, often in the form of parody of other contemporary sayings. They make up a genre of "attitude apparel" of a different sort from that of "Successories." "Time flies when you don't know what you're doing"("Time flies when you're having fun"). "If you love something, set it free, and if it doesn't come back to you, hunt it down and kill it" (a parody of the more saccharine "If you love something set it free, and if it doesn't come back to you, it was never yours to begin with").

While some people are walking around this world sporting Successories "attitude apparel" (T-shirts) bearing helpful, upbeat slogans like "Attitude is everything," "Make It Happen," and "Whatever It Takes," others are sauntering around in what might be christened "bad-attitude apparel": "I'd like to help you out. Which way did you come in?" "Everyone needs to believe in something. I believe I'll have another beer." "I wish you were a beer." "It's not whether you win or lose, it's how you look playing the game." "The one who dies with the most toys wins." "Experience is what you get when you didn't get what you wanted." "Rules were made to be broken."

Practical tips for daily living are offered by the following T-shirt slogans. "Everyone wants to go to heaven, but no one wants to die."

"Never try to teach a pig to sing—it wastes your time and annoys the pig." "Perfect paranoia is perfect awareness." "Never attribute to malice what can be adequately explained by stupidity."[14]

Proverbs Subverting Office Optimism

While some people are decorating their office walls with attractive framed posters encouraging commitment, enthusiasm, and opportunity, others are standing at copy machines running off "get real" subversive office wisdom. They are perpetrators of yet another source of subversive contemporary wisdom: photocopier folklore. Photocopier proverbs can be observed by walking unannounced into any office (almost any office, at least) and inspecting the walls, desks, and bulletin boards for the wisdom of the office sages. They subvert traditional wisdom's pairing of hard work with positive outcomes based on their observation of situations in which the best-laid plans are upset by other people's mistakes, technological error, and the unpredictability of daily life.

Wry observations on the difficulties of working with other human beings and computers are encapsulated in the following photocopier proverbs. "Nothing is impossible for the man who doesn't have to do it himself." "It's difficult to soar with eagles when you work with turkeys." "The only difference between this place and the Titanic is they had a band." "The rat race is over; the rats won." "When I'm right, no one remembers. When I'm wrong, no one forgets." "Some minds are like concrete—all mixed up and permanently set."

The fast pace of technological change in the business world is bemoaned in the following: "Just when I knew all the answers, they changed all the questions." "Never let anything mechanical know you are in a hurry." "To err is human. To really foul things up requires a computer."

A proverb collected in Foster City, California (1986): "No amount of planning will ever replace dumb luck." "Old age and treachery will overcome youth and skill" subverts American culture's fairy-tale norms in which the youngest/best motif typically triumphs. The traditional American respect for diversity of opinion is subverted by the photocopier admonition "Be tolerant of those who disagree with you; after all, they have a right to their stupid opinions."[15]

The proverb parodist walks on the grass, writes on the walls, and tramples the no-trespassing sign posted on the well-manicured lawn of traditional wisdom to the end that no tidbit of self-serious traditional wisdom may be left unscathed. Proverb parody deserves the preacher's notice precisely because of its defiant irreverence, its tinkering with the wording, subverting the original meaning of time-honored sayings. Christian preachers, in our mission to subvert cynical, materialistic aspects of traditional wisdom, can learn a lesson from the parodist who boldly goes where he is not supposed to go.

Fulfilling that mission means a new alertness to the proverbial activity of ordering and subverting which flourishes all around us. Sometimes cynical proverbs subvert hopeful proverbs with an echo of Qohelet's pricking the balloon of traditional wisdom, and the preacher can acknowledge that life sometimes gives us warrant for a bad attitude. "One door closes and another door closes" is a pessimistic proverb subverting the sunnier Irish proverb "God never shuts a door but he opens another."[16] "Behind every silver lining there's a dark cloud" subverts the more sanguine "Behind every dark cloud there's a silver lining."[17] A billboard for a building contractor in an affluent suburban area depicts a spacious home in a pastoral setting. As its caption is a proverb parody that ought to annoy every preacher driving by: "You *can* buy happiness."

Sometimes deeper proverbs subvert shallow proverbs and the preacher can commend them for their insight. "Life begins at 40" subverts the culture of youth worship of our society. "Life is short, pray hard" subverts the athletic-shoe proverb that depicts us all as sentenced to spend our lives pounding pavements in increasingly expensive pairs of sneakers: "Life is short, play hard."

Proverbs Venting Anger at Dominant Groups

We have seen how the most pernicious social function of proverbs is in oppressing society's least powerful groups. Proverbs also function to help an oppressed group express its anger and assess the faults of a dominant group. The proverb "Women have many faults" is the basis for the misogynist rhyme from 1727, which begins with a gender change.

> We men have many faults;
> Poor women have but two—
> There's nothing good they say,
> There's nothing good they do.

So feminist graffiti of the 1970s , spreading in time to T-shirts and buttons, produced this popular subversive version:

Women's faults are many;
Men have only two:
Everything they say
And everything they do.[18]

Two proverbs subversive of male power come from African-American women. "Rooster makes more racket than do de hen what lay de egg." and "Mens! You can dress 'em up, but you can't take 'em out."[19] Several proverbs ascribed to native Americans subvert the white settlers' claim to moral superiority by characterizing them in unflattering ways. "No Indian ever sold his daughter for a name." "The Indian scalps his enemy; the paleface skins his friends." "The Indian takes his dog to heaven; the paleface sends his brother to hell." "There will be hungry palefaces so long as there is any Indian land to swallow."[20]

The function of proverbs to express criticism of a dominant group and dissatisfaction with their role in life is operative in proverbs of the slave quarters. While slave owners were quoting the Anglo-American proverb "A watched pot never boils," their slaves were coining the subversive proverbial variant "An empty pot never boils!" Other proverbs that lent themselves to criticism of masters are: "The black snake knows the way to the hen's nest." "Waitin' on the table is a powerful way to get up an appetite." "The mousetrap doesn't go to sleep." "Crow and corn cain't grow in de same field." "A robin's song ain't pretty to a worm." "Tain't much difference between a hornet and a yella-jacket when dey both under your clothes." "The white man knows when you're right; he sees, but acts like he don't." "You can't hold a man down without staying down with him," a proverb attributed to Booker T. Washington.[21]

Not only do proverbs function as vents for anger and criticism of dominant groups, they also encapsulate the identity of the suppressed group, both their positive and their defeated sentiments.

The Korean proverb "When whales fight, the shrimp's back is broken" reflects the buffeting of their country by larger competing nations.[22] A proverb that subverts racial prejudice in this country is "The blacker the berry the sweeter the juice." An African-American woman, born around 1905, explained the proverb in the following way: "There was class among Black folks based on color. Lighter skinned people were considered better, and lighter skinned Blacks got the first and best jobs. Old folks said it [this proverb] to boast [sic] the self-esteem of darker Black children, especially girls. They were saying, "Hold your head up."[23] Mary McLeod Bethune, African-American activist and educator, used to go into segregated white stores and demand to try on hats, brushing aside shocked white clerks' refusals with": Do you know who I am? I am Mary McLeod Bethune! From her lips Marian Wright Edelman, founder of the Children's Defense Fund, remembers first hearing this proverb, "The blacker the berry, the sweeter the juice."[24]

Sadly, this proverb is subverted by the voice of painful experience "The blacker the berry the sweeter the juice, but if you're too damn black it ain't no use!"[25]

The well-known slogan of the manufacturers of Virginia Slims cigarettes, "You've come a long way, baby" became a motto of the women's liberation movement of the 1970s. After the failure of the Equal Rights Amendment in 1982 a T-shirt appeared bearing the words, "I Haven't Come a Long Way."[26]

This dynamic of the subversion of a subversive proverb by a pessimistic parody expresses the struggle of members of suppressed groups between self-esteem and abiding cultural prejudice. A proverb that subverts racism perpetrated and observed is "Black is beautiful!" The Reverend Dr. Martin Luther King, Jr., launched a poster campaign based on these words in 1967, but Stokely Carmichael had used the phrase at a Memphis civil rights rally in 1966. It may have its origins in Song of Solomon 1:5, "I am black but comely." A related rallying cry is "Say it loud: I'm Black and I'm proud!" (James Brown, 1968; 30).

Proverbs Building Community Solidarity and Self-Esteem

The tradition of using proverbs to build community solidarity and esteem stretches back to the sayings of the slavery days. Proverbs were used by American slaves to survive their inhumane conditions. One of their functions was to teach survival skills. "You've got eyes to see and wisdom not to see" (an injunction to slaves not to tell on each other). "Every eye shut ain't asleep." "Ol' Massa takes care of himself, but we've got to go to God." "Don't crow 'til you get out of the woods—they might be beating behind the last tree" (don't be careless about talking to people you see until you get to the Underground Railroad). "The Field Mouse lies still when Sparrow-hawk sails." Other sayings issue the warning that good fortune is fragile amid the realities of an often hostile life. "Watch out when you're getting all you want. Fattening hogs ain't in luck." "The north wind knows all the cracks in the house." Avoidance of potentially dangerous situations is recommended by "Any dog knows better than to chew on a razor," and "If you fool with trash, it'll get in your eyes." "Quagmires don't hang out no signs."

Proverbs convey another axiom, crucial to African-American survival in the days of slavery: the hope for justice. "Raindrops can't tell broadcloth from jeans." "It rains and every man feels it someday." The validity of justice institutions of white domination is challenged in "All the justice in the world ain't fastened up in the courthouse." "If slavery isn't wrong, nothing is wrong."

The attractiveness of the prospect of death compared to the slave's life is an incentive to take risks forbidden by the dominant group. In an existence in which, even before the physical body is destroyed, "Dreams die first," "The quicker the death, the quicker the heaven." "You might as well die with the chills as with the fever" (refers to a common plantation malady, but also that one might as well get killed trying to escape as to remain a slave and die in slavery).

Proverbs were used in the days of slavery to foster group identity, crucial to survival. "Don't forget where you came from." "Be proud of what you are." "Sometimes the runt pig beats the whole litter growing." "The pine tree doesn't fear the frost." Several contemporary proverbs of African-American origin foster group identity by subverting the devaluation of a people, challenging materialism and injustice. "If you don't have the best of everything, make the best of everything you have." "Keeping up with the Joneses will keep you down." And "Injustice anywhere is a threat to justice everywhere," "The eye-for-an-eye philosophy leaves everybody blind," "Unless a man has found the thing he will die for, he is not fit to live"—three sayings coined by Martin Luther King, Jr. (1963). A proverb attributed to Eldridge Cleaver (1968) challenges his own people to continue to work for justice. "You're either part of the solution or part of the problem."[27] A saying with relevance for the day-to-day struggles of African-American women is "Make a way out of no way," used by Alice Walker as a description of her mother, to whom she dedicates her book *The Third Life of Grange Copeland*.[28]

Proverbs Expressing
a Community's Core Beliefs

A body of sayings exists that places these observations about life in a theological context. What are called cultural axioms in secular terms are better known as "core beliefs" with reference to African-American communities of faith. Core beliefs are "the bedrock attitudes that govern all deliberate behavior and relationships and also all spontaneous responses to crises." Core beliefs express the community's "trust in the Creator as evidenced by their ability to cope with their life experiences."[29] Taken together, these core beliefs make up a worldview that Nicholas Cooper-Lewter and Henry H. Mitchell call "soul theology." Core beliefs are expressed by brief sayings and lines from scripture, hymns, and spirituals and are used proverbially in the challenging situations of the community's life. Several core beliefs concern the nature of God, while still others express convictions about the nature of the people of God.

The providence of God is expressed in the saying "It is God who drives away the flies from the cow who has no tail." The justice of God: "The Good Book say you gonna reap what you sow." The omnipotence of God: "My God is so high you can't git over him." The omniscience of God: "He who knows and sees all, the before and behind, is omniscient." The goodness of God and creation: "Well, I wouldn't take nothin' for my journey now." The grace of God: "Swing low, sweet chariot, comin' for to carry me home." Alongside these core beliefs about God are some affirmations about people. The equality of persons: "No big I's and little you's." The uniqueness of persons: "The good Lord done come by here and blessed my soul." The importance of community as the family of God: "Because we are here, I am." The perseverance of people—"Keep your hand on the plow, and hang on!"

The theological norms or core beliefs of these proverbial expressions serve a pastoral role in the community, affirming the goodness of God in divine governance of the community. They also serve a subversive function, expressing a standard of judgment on the wider community's attitudes and practices.

Several "core beliefs" are subversions of the beliefs of dominant cultural wisdom. The core belief in the omnipotence of God subverts a secular definition of power as generated and sustained by human beings. This is expressed in a number of lines from gospel songs, hymns, and spirituals that function as proverbs in commenting on daily life.[30] "My God is so high, you can't git over him; He's so low, you can't git under him; He's so wide, you can't git around him." This God guarantees that "Trouble don't last always." "Ride on, King Jesus, no man can hinder thee!" "He's got the whole world in his hands."[31]

The omnipotence of God in relation to daily life is expressed in phrases like "The Lord will make a way somehow," "He opens doors for me, doors I cannot see," or "Jesus, build a fence all around me." Gospel songs affirm that "He is able," and that "God can do anything but fail." For African-American communities of faith, both historically and today, the existence of evil deeds and evildoers does not lead to despair. Rather, it makes a belief in the providence of an omnipotent God mandatory (158).

The grace of God is another core belief which, from the time of life in the slave quarters, has subverted the hopelessness of life by strengthening black communities' faith. The hymn "Amazing Grace," whose words were composed by Englishman and former slave-ship captain turned evangelist John Newton, is a favorite hymn of the black churches, especially the line " 'Twas grace that brought me safe thus far" (45). Another popular, grace-filled hymn is Joseph Scriven's "What a friend we have in Jesus, all our sins and griefs to bear"(81).

While core beliefs make affirmations about God's omnipotence and grace, they also state convictions about the people of God. A key affirmation is the persistence of the people. The black community's notion of perseverance subverts that of majority culture, which views it as a means of winning out over others. Majority culture has sayings like "Winners never quit and quitters never win." "But victory in the Soul community has nothing to do with defeating someone else; its sole goal is to survive intact. The commitment not to quit is not against anybody; it opposes only those who would hurt and oppress"(146).

The African-based belief system, reflected in the culture of the slave era and today, places high value on patience and perseverance. Africans used the tortoise to teach patience and perseverance. A Yoruba proverb declares, "The snail climbs the tree carefully and slowly." This statement is typical of a whole body of wisdom praising the virtues of being watchful, slow, and steady, teaching that steadiness succeeds where quickness often fails. Many American blacks today quote the old saying "The race is not to the swift nor the strong, but to him that endureth to the end" (a collation of Eccl. 9:11 and Matt. 24:13).

"Keep your hand on the plow [and] hold on!" "Cheer the weary traveler, along the heavenly way"(142). "Keep inchin' along, like a ol' inchworm"—in preparation for when "Jesus is coming by and by." "I shall not, I shall not be moved, Just like a tree, planted by the waters" (Ps. 1:3). "Walk together, children, don't you get weary; There's a great camp meetin' in the Promised Land" (Gal. 6:9). The theme of not turning back sounds in "I'll never turn back no more, no more." "I have decided to follow Jesus; No turning back, no turning back"(145).

Clearly this notion of perseverance is different from the secular admonitions whose goal is to "See you at the top!" Perseverance of the soul is, rather, a reminder that, because of the providential guidance of God, there is no place for long-lasting discouragement, and so the community presses on in faith and hope (147).

PART THREE
SERMONS
ON PROVERBS

8

The Proof
Is in the Pudding:
Preaching Proverbs That
Create Order

SERMON MODEL A—"THE ROVING SPOTLIGHT"

The "Roving Spotlight" model is based on the quality essential to what makes a proverb a proverb: its rhetorical intention to be placed in particular contemporary situations to act as a wise, interpretive word. The "roving spotlight" is well suited to preaching proverbs that strike the reader as incontestably good advice drawn from human experience that resonates with aspects of his own. Many, though by no means all, of these are antithetical proverbs in which the first half of the proverb sets forth foolish behavior to be avoided, the second half wise behavior to be espoused. Besides its usefulness in preaching antithetical one-verse proverbs, this model also lends itself to preaching on two-verse antithetical proverb pairs. The movement in this model is often from negative to positive, warning to recommendation (Prov. 14:20–21; 18:12).

One's mind is set to work using the proverb like a searchlight scanning one's own and one's congregation's life experiences and observations, as well as those of the men and women and children who people the Bible and church and secular history for situations in which this proverb would be a wise, illuminating word and then training a spotlight on them. Some themes dealt with by such proverbs include the superiority of wisdom to material possessions and of humility to pride, the distinction between the values and fates of the wise and the fool, the importance of compassionate treatment of the poor, truthfulness, cheerfulness, relinquishment of grudges, fear of the Lord, thoughtful, prudent speech, and wise and timely rebuke.

In our use of Jesus' subversive proverbs and aphorisms to shape the identity of a counter-order community, the "roving spotlight" and the "sometimes, but not always" models can be useful. A roving spotlight sermon could be preached on the aphorism "Are grapes gathered from thorns, or figs from thistles?" or "A city built on a hill cannot be hid." A sometimes, but not always sermon could be preached on "Those who find their life will lose it, and those who lose their life for my sake will find it" (Matt. 10:39).

A given proverb may lend itself to a number of sermonic approaches. Choosing among them in a given context is a function of the wisdom of the preacher as sage.

Proverbs that lend themselves to the roving spotlight model include:

Proverbs 6:27–28
10:6–12, 16–21, 23, 24, 28–29, 31–32
11:1, 2, 3, 5, 6, 11, 12, 13, 14, 17, 18, 20, 24, 25, 27, 30
12:1, 2, 3, 5, 6, 11, 12, 15, 18, 20, 22, 25, 26
13:1, 11, 12, 13, 14, 15, 20
14:10, 12, 20–21, 26–27, 31, 32, 34
15:4, 8, 9, 10, 12, 13, 14, 15, 16, 17, 21, 23, 26, 28, 31–33
16:3, 6, 8, 16, 18–20, 22, 25
17:1, 3, 5, 9, 14, 17, 22, 24
18:2, 21, 24
19:1, 2, 3, 8, 16, 17, 21, 22
20:3, 7, 17, 22
21:2, 11, 13, 15, 16, 23, 30
22:1, 9, 22–23
23:4–5, 10–11, 17–18
24:3–6, 10–12, 17–18, 23–26, 27
25:11, 12, 15, 16, 18, 26, 28
26:12, 17, 20, 21, 27
27:1, 2, 5, 21
28:1, 5, 6, 10, 13, 15–16, 23, 27
29:1, 2, 6–8, 23, 25
30:32

The sermon that follows makes an explicit connection between Wisdom in Proverbs and the Wisdom revealed to us in Jesus Christ. The possibilities for such connections are myriad, but not necessary in preaching from proverbial texts from the Hebrew Scriptures. This sermon would be good news even without the explicit connection of Jesus with Wisdom, a connection that could be made via hymns, prayers, and litanies that compose the worship context of the sermon.

SERMON:
Hope Deferred Makes the Heart Sick:
"What Are You Waiting For?"

> *Texts:* "Hope deferred makes the heart sick, but a desire fulfilled is a tree of life." (Prov. 13:2)
>
> The story of the disciples on the road to Emmaus. (Luke 24:13–31)
>
> *Context:* Communion Sunday

Every summer the third week of August, our family goes to Rehoboth Beach, Delaware, to enjoy the sun and the surf. The summer of 1995 Hurricane Felix made the winds so strong they ripped our kites to shreds, the waves so high and the riptide so strong that we were allowed in only knee-deep and, for a couple of days, not at all. One of those afternoons, while everyone else was napping or playing monopoly, I found myself wandering down Rehoboth Avenue staring idly in the windows of T-shirt stores and yearningly through the windows of the Candy Kitchens that crop up on every corner. I passed a little storefront that had a big chalkboard slate propping its door open. Written on it in yellow chalk were the words: "Questions about Your Future? Palm Reading $10." There was a line of about ten people waiting to go in. Inside was a woman sitting at a small round table with a chair across from her.

Now, as a minister it is my duty to explore the things that people in this country put their faith in besides the Christian gospel. I have to know my competition. Besides, I was bored, and besides, I had one or two nagging questions about my future just like anybody else. So I got in line behind the others, debating whether I would really shell out $10 to see my future etched in the wrinkles on my hand.

What about you? Don't you have a question or two about your future? You get in line with me. We have time to watch and listen in on what's going on inside and decide if it's worth our money. As each person's turn comes, he sits across from the palm reader; she takes his hand in hers and reads his love line (romantic prospects or lack thereof), his life line (forecasting how old he'll be when he dies), and his travel line (if he will win a trip to Europe). And then, finally, she looks at the person across from her intently and asks, "Do you have any questions about your future?" This is the moment it gets interesting. Because this is when the person attached to the palm, reveals his or her heart's desire. "Do you have any questions about your future?" One by one, with troubled faces, people ask things like, "Will I meet someone soon?" "Will this separation from my spouse be permanent?" "Will I get the job I want?" "Will I relocate?" "Will my brother get parole?" "Will I have grandchildren?"

A person's heart's desire is how a person fills in the blank in the sentence: "If only . . . then I would be satisfied." "If only . . . I would feel good about my life." Your heart's desire is what you are waiting for, hoping for, so intensely that it blinds you to the fact that the deepest desire of all human hearts is already fulfilled at the center of your life.

Several people are still ahead of us in line, but your turn will be coming up soon. When the palm reader is looking at you and asking, "Do you have any questions about your future? What is your heart's desire?" What will you say?

As I watch the worried faces of those seeking knowledge of the future and see the worry lighten and lift if they hear the answer they're hoping for, a proverb occurs to me: "Hope deferred makes the heart sick, but a desire fulfilled is a tree of life" (Prov. 13:12). As we wait together in this ever-shortening line, my mind begins to rove over people I know and know of, who might fall into line with us, each with a nagging question about what the future holds, each preoccupied with a hope deferred, each ignoring the desire fulfilled at the center of their lives, if only they would grasp it.

"Hope deferred makes the heart sick." I was once conducting a service as a guest minister at a small rural church. The sanctuary was so small that I could read the expressions on the faces of the people on the back pew. I had noticed a woman on the back row whose face looked very attentive and at the same time very troubled. It came time for Communion. I blessed the elements and handed trays of bread to the ushers to serve to people in the pews. An usher got to the back row and stood next to her offering her the tray of bread, but as he held it out to her, she shook her head and put both hands up in a gesture of refusal such as one uses to ward off a blow. She happened to catch my eye at that moment, and I raised my eyebrows as if to ask, "What gives?" She shook her head again. After the service, she waited to be last to go past and shake my hand. "You noticed I didn't take Communion. I am new to this area and this church. I haven't been to church for a long time. I am trying to give up smoking and make some other changes in my life and I want to be sure I can make them stick before I feel worthy to take Communion. Do you understand?" I thought for a long moment and then said to her, "I'm so glad that you came this morning. And I have some good news for you that I believe is true, though it's hard for all of us to grasp. It is that the gift of Jesus' death and life for us doesn't need to be earned. That means you're waiting for something you already have." She gave me a puzzled look and said simply, "I'll be back next week." What would this woman's answer be to the question "Do you have any questions about your future?" Through the years the image of her holding her hands up to ward off the body of Christ given for her is still clear in my mind's eye.

"Hope deferred makes the heart sick." What is she waiting for?

A couple of weeks ago I was riding my stationary bike, one of my least favorite things to do in life, but which I do faithfully because I hope that someday I'll be glad I did. To avoid spending the whole twenty minutes looking at my watch and wishing it were over, I was channel-surfing in search of mindless entertainment to make the time fly by. I was in luck! There was a Barbara Walters interview with Burt Reynolds, and it wasn't even a current one, it was from 1978! I congratulated myself on my good fortune and pedaled with renewed vigor. This is perfect! No moral lessons, no sermon material here.

Then Burt started talking about his relationship with his dad, the sheriff in a small Southern town, beloved by everyone, but strict with his son, who respected and feared him and yearned for signs of tenderness and approval from him. But it was not to be. Says Burt, "Our family lived by two simple rules: No crying. No hugging." He went on, "There's a saying in the South that 'no man is a man until his father tells him he is,' and I hadn't yet gotten that message from my father. I kept hoping someday I would hear it."

In the meantime, Burt's hopes of being a professional football player were destroyed by an injury and his hopes of being an actor were growing dim. They told him he looked like Marlon Brando, but that he didn't have any talent. A few bit parts in his twenties left him at age thirty-two the best-known unknown in Hollywood. "Hope deferred makes the heart sick."

Then his marriage to Judy Carne hit the rocks. This would be the first divorce in his family. He remembers staring at the phone, knowing he had to call home and break the news but afraid that he would get his dad instead of his mother, and yet wanting more than anything to hear his father's voice—standing there, staring at the phone, not able to will himself to pick it up. What would Burt's answer be in this moment to the question: "Do you have any questions about your future?" "Hope deferred makes the heart sick, but a desire fulfilled is a tree of life." What do you suppose he is waiting for?

This proverb was written by an anonymous Israelite sage after observing many different scenarios in which people lived lives of waiting, hoping, all the while their desire fulfilled, God's presence, lay at the heart of their lives. It was used by sages after the exile to address the nation's waiting for their heart's desire, deferring their hopes, until they were sick at heart. The wise teachers (sages) of the Israelite people after the exile in Jerusalem heard many conversations that began and ended with "If only we had a king again. . . . " "If only we had the Temple again. . . . " "If only there weren't so many difficult choices facing our young people!" "If only we had direction!" "If only God had not withdrawn from us!" If only God would restore to us the glory of the former days. Maybe God will. But when? The sages used this proverb in a multitude of mundane situations and conversations to challenge and to give solace, with the question: Why are we waiting sick at heart for a presence that already lies at the heart of our nation?

"Happy are those who find wisdom, and those who get understanding, for her income is better than silver, and her revenue better than gold. She is more precious than jewels, and nothing you desire can compare with her. . . . She is a tree of life to those who lay hold of her; those who hold her fast are called happy" (Prov. 3:13–18).

What are you waiting for? the sages of Israel asked their people. Isn't God's Wisdom here, accessible in our midst every day? "Does not wisdom call, and does not understanding raise her voice? On the heights, beside the way, at the crossroads"—in the marketplace, the field, the home, beside the hearth—"she takes her stand; beside the gates in front of the town, at the entrance of the portals she cries out" (8:1–3). Why are you moaning that God is distant when Wisdom is here? She brings the answer to our every question about the future—that God is here, guiding us in each passing moment.

"Hope deferred makes the heart sick." Luke shaped his account of the Emmaus road encounter to emphasize the reality of the resurrection and the presence of the risen One in the community, because some circles in the early church were so busy scanning the skies that they had no eyes for the present. When will he return? When? So Luke invites his readers to see themselves in the disciples, walking heads down, steps dragging, the way we always walk when our hearts are sick with preoccupation about our deferred hopes. What do you suppose they're waiting for?

When our nation gets that defeatist gait, and church people start complaining that we have no leadership in this country, that it's so hard to raise children in this country, that there is no moral compass in this country, what on earth are we waiting for?

"Hope deferred makes the heart sick." I think of a vicar, a man of moral integrity, who delivered moving homilies, who visited faithfully in the homes of the parish, with a special knack for cheering the homebound elderly. But, for hidden reasons of his own, for several years he had been living out a sort of grim-duty version of his calling, getting through it, putting in twelve-hour days, without taking a day off—though that was something his congregation believed its pastors needed to do—living for the day he retired.

In both private and public his refrain was "I can't wait until I retire. . . . I can spend time in my garden, take my wife out to dinner once a week, take my grandson to soccer matches. I can't wait until I retire." His people wondered what he was waiting for. They wondered why he couldn't build some of that gracious leisure time he yearned for into his present life. It hurt them that their pastor's definition of Christian ministry was enduring their irksome company for two more years, until he could escape from them and, at long last, enjoy himself.

Their vicar retired. He and his wife moved into a cottage in a nearby community. Then, just a few months later, he suffered a stroke that affected his ability to walk and speak. With therapy he is walking short distances and is regaining his speech. He sits much of the day in a recliner by the front door of his home, a table with a telephone on it by his side. He may be sitting there right now. What do you think he is waiting for?

"Hope deferred makes the heart sick." In the heat of an inner-city July, Chris Hamilton, age thirteen, dabbed paint on a mural outside the Isabel Miller Community Center in Camden, New Jersey. Chris is a participant in the Banner Project, a program begun in 1989, which teaches its young participants conflict resolution through music, painting, and storytelling. Begun in the school districts of Philadelphia and Pittsburgh, it has expanded to Camden, offering day camps for city youth at the city's five community centers. The mural Chris designed is called "My Friends." It shows children in a pastoral scene: rolling green hills, lush trees, the sun, a rainbow. He carefully chooses three skin tones for the group of friends, dark brown, beige, and reddish brown. One of his counselors asks him, "What do you see when you look at the mural?" He replies, "No violence. No killing. Peace on earth."[1] Hopes like this by children should not have to be deferred. What are we adults who profess our commitment to peace in the family of God waiting for?

As we live out our "if only" days, looking yearningly to the day when our heart's desire will be fulfilled, our proverb shines an interrogatory light in our eyes and asks us the disconcerting question: "What are you waiting for?" For the Israelite people, it wasn't just king, or Temple, but the presence of a God they feared had drawn away from them. Yet all the while that they are waiting for signs of God's renewed favor, a tree is planted in the midst of their lives.

Throughout the book of Proverbs, Wisdom is referred to not only as helping God in the creation of the world, but as "a tree of life to those who lay hold of her; those who hold her fast are called happy" (Prov. 3:18). Holding her fast at life's center, we become like her. As the psalmist sings, we become like trees planted by streams of water, fruitful, unwithered (from Ps. 1:3); we become, as the African-American proverb describes, "pine trees [that] need not fear the frost."

When we lay hold on Wisdom, the tree of life, she casts a critical eye at our heart's desire. She is not just a tree, she is a master gardener. If our heart's desire is self-centered or materialistic, Wisdom uproots it so wise desires can grow in its place. If our heart's desire, however laudable, is withered by the heat of life, she comforts us and inspires with hopes. If our heart's desire is a noble goal, but one that needs lots of cultivation, we have her help right now in working toward it.

The deepest desire of our human hearts—for God to love us and never leave us, to be present to guide us whatever waves roll up on the shore, is fulfilled. Wisdom's tree of life is planted by streams of water at the depths of our lives.

"A desire fulfilled is a tree of life." Chris puts the finishing touches on his mural of many-hued friends, and then he joins hands with other youth and their adult counselor in reciting the Banner Project's motto: "I am somebody, and I am special. You are somebody, and you are special. We are somebodies and we are special. Peace." The beginning of a desire fulfilled blooms in the city in that moment.

After staring, staring at that telephone on the table, dreading calling home to tell the news of his pending divorce, Burt Reynolds says, he finally picked up the phone, dialed his parents' number with shaking hands, and, thank God, got his mother on the phone. "Mom, Judy and I are getting a divorce. No, it's final. Mom, tell him I'm sorry. Tell him I've failed again and that I'm sorry." "Then," he says, "I heard this other voice on the phone. 'Come home,' my father said, 'and let me tell you about all the times I've failed in my life'."

The invitation should have come years before. Parents shouldn't make their children wait to receive the blessing of a love that stays steady through success and failure. But whenever the blessing comes, it is a gift of God's Wisdom that we've allowed to break through our barriers. It is a desire fulfilled, and it is a tree of life.

Our retired vicar is sitting by the telephone; his hopes for a healthy, carefree retirement have been dealt a blow. But he has a desire fulfilled despite his physical limitations. The presence of God's wisdom has rekindled his joy in ministry, even from an armchair. Of course he has his bad days. But he no longer spends every day waiting for joy. Instead, he spends much of his time on the phone, in a telephone ministry to shut-ins. He still has his knack for brightening their day like nobody else, for sharing the joy of the God he has served and continues to serve. He's probably talking to someone right now, sharing the good news that "a desire fulfilled is a tree of life."

The disciples on the road to Emmaus, yearning for guidance and comfort, in a word for wisdom, are joined by a fellow traveler whom they do not recognize, but from whom they cannot bear to be parted. "Come in and share a meal with us," they beg him. And Jesus makes himself known to them in the breaking of the bread. Thus

Luke assures the church of his age and ours that the Lord, Wisdom-in-person, is in our midst, our guide and companion in whatever disappointments and challenges face us today. "A desire fulfilled is a tree of life." Wisdom is a tree of life. Those who hold her fast are called happy.

I do hope that our friend with the attentive, troubled face is worshiping this morning in that small rural church. I know that she is worshiping here. I invite you to join me in hoping that as Christ offers wisdom and comfort to her in sermon, prayer, music, and sacrament, she will not put up her arms to ward off so great a blessing, but will open them to embrace the gift of God's presence. "A desire fulfilled is a tree of life."

Well, what are you waiting for? It's our turn at the palm reader's table. Our chance has finally come to find the answer to our most pressing question about our future, whether our heart's desire will be fulfilled or not.

I think I'm going to put my ten-dollar bill back in my pocket and stroll on down the street. Maybe I'll use it to buy a T-shirt or a quarter pound of chocolate peanut butter fudge. Then I'm going to walk on down toward the ocean to see how high the waves are getting, in the company of a God who, in all the storms of an unpredictable life, loves each one of us and will never leave us. What about you?

SERMON MODEL B—"SOMETIMES, BUT NOT ALWAYS"

This model is based on the nature of the proverb as a partial generalization, appropriate for certain situations in contemporary life, but not for all of them. When preaching a "Sometimes, but Not Always" proverbs sermon, the preacher as sage first exercises her wisdom in determining a constellation of contemporary situations in which the proverb is an ethically illuminating word. She then suggests a constellation of experiences in which the proverb would not be helpful, which might even call for a seemingly opposite interpretation. The model emphasizes both the helpfulness of a proverb and its limitations.

Texts from proverbs that lend themselves to the "sometimes, but not always" model are those about which, when one reads them, one thinks, "Yes, in some cases that is undoubtedly true, but in other situations . . . " Some suggestions of texts that lend themselves to this model are:

Proverbs 10:10, 15, 28
      11:8
      12:16
      13:3, 10
      14:13, 16, 29, 30
      15:1, 5, 18, 22
      16:25, 32
      17:27
      19:4, 7, 11, 19, 20
      21:5
      25:20
      26:17
      29:11, 15

SERMON:
A Soft Answer Turns Away Wrath:
"Sometimes, but Not Always"
      Text: "A soft answer turns away wrath, but a harsh word stirs up anger." (Prov. 15:1)

You're tired. It has been an irritating day. Another household member comes in from school or work, in an equally irritable mood, and an encounter ensues, tailor-made to push your anger buttons. You snap back. The other party makes an angry exit, slamming the door as an exclamation point. As you sit slumped at the kitchen table, the words of the sages from Proverbs come to mind: "A soft answer turns away wrath, but a harsh word stirs up anger."

The wise men and women of the Israelites, called sages, had observed countless occasions when the strategy of choosing a soft answer had turned away wrath. The sages responsible for collecting the sayings in our biblical book of Proverbs probably lived in the time after the Israelites' exile to Babylon, when they had returned to Palestine and were trying to rebuild their community life in an authority vacuum. The twin bulwarks of community stability, monarchy and Temple, had both crumbled. This was a time in which harsh words and wrath abounded, over land rights, over marriages outside the community. There was no single unifying authority figure.

So the sages envisioned God's attribute of wisdom as a Wise

Woman, co-creator with God of order in the human and natural worlds, author of wise sayings, stationing herself at the busiest cross-roads of community life, speaking proverbs that beckoned the young to enter on the path of wisdom that leads to life. What kind of life did those proverbs command? Moderation in food and drink, hard work, respect for elders and the poor, sexual morality. And one more cru-cial thing: the wise use of speech. Woman Wisdom has sixty sayings (in Proverbs 10—22) that deal with the wise use of speech. Many, but not all of them, commend the quality of gentleness as a hallmark of wise speech. Avoiding harsh words and anger was one way she rec-ommended for keeping community order and social peace (shalom). The survival of the community depended on it.

Jesus, among his other roles, was a teacher of wisdom, a sage. Af-ter the resurrection, the early church affirmed, as we do today, that Jesus is Wisdom-in-person, the presence of God among us guiding us in the wise use of language. When we look to his example as sage, we find his language strategies informed by this proverb from Woman Wisdom. As subversive as he was much of the time, he knew there was a time and a place for a soft answer. To the woman caught in adultery, about to be stoned by a group of religious professionals, he said, "Neither do I condemn you. Go your way, and from now on do not sin again" (John 8:11). To a criminal hanging on a cross next to his, he offers the words "Truly I tell you, today you will be with me in Paradise" (Luke 23:43).

Looking back at our own lives, we can think of times we wish we had chosen the soft answer with spouses, friends, children. History sometimes bears witness to the wisdom of the soft-answer strategy. Dur-ing the long, hot summer months of 1789 in Philadelphia, the members of the Constitutional Convention met behind locked doors, arguing, discussing, wrangling, and debating. Benjamin Franklin, that master proverb collector and coiner, frequently acted as their peacemaker. A disagreement arose over representation of smaller states versus larger states. The conflict escalated, threatening to derail the Convention, with its work unfinished. In the thick of the fray, the master aphorist rose slowly to his feet. "When a broad table is to be made and the edges of the planks do not fit, the artisan takes a little from both and makes a good joint," he suggested quietly. His proverbial com-ment had the effect of dispelling the turmoil in the room. Hot tem-pers cooled, and delegates were able to hear Franklin's suggestion that a committee be formed to try to arrange a compromise that would satisfy everyone.[2] The Convention subsequently produced the Constitution, a model in such compromise.

Wise speech. The sages defined it as speech that was based on respect for God, or the fear of the Lord, and the authority of the sages. Wise speech was a fountain of life in home, school, marketplace, field, and court. But they recognized that not all speech is wise speech. When spouted by fools, those who are wise in their own eyes, it becomes false, ferocious babbling. Then wise people need to choose a strategy of harsh words to counter harmful speech.

A case in point is the current spate of talk shows whose staple is confrontation, conducted in a coliseum atmosphere. A young male guest on a TV show about secret crushes was stunned to find that his "secret admirer" was a young man of his acquaintance. Feeling that it is more acceptable to be a murderer than a homosexual in this society, the young man went to his "secret admirer's" home and shot him in the chest. One talk show critic's comment was, "The only problem most talk show hosts have with the murder is that it didn't happen on the air." (Roger Ailes, quoted in "Are Talk Shows out of Control?" *TV Guide,* April 1–7, 1995.)

Would the sages of Israel have disapproved of this harsh word against media morals? Hardly! These same sages who said, "A soft answer turns away wrath," also said, "The one who rebukes boldly makes peace" (Prov. 10:10). "Like . . . an ornament of gold is a wise rebuke to a listening ear" (25:12). The sages, speaking on behalf of Wisdom, were quick to affirm that wise words aren't always soft words.

Some of the most famous leaders in history have known that wise speech means choosing harsh words for harsh times. One of Winston Churchill's favorite sayings was a variation he coined on the familiar proverb "Make hay while the sun shines." His version, in the context of stirring up the English people to stand firm against Hitler, was "Make hell while the sun shines!"[3]

Jesus' language usage reflects Woman Wisdom's appreciation of the positive value of rebuke more than her strategy of the soft answer. He uses proverbs, and words in general, not in a traditional way to smooth things over, but in a subversive way, to stir them up, to heighten tensions and propel people to the point of decision. When the Pharisees criticize his disciples for eating without washing their hands, Jesus goes on the offensive: "There is nothing outside a person that by going in can defile, but the things that come out are what defile" (Mark 7:15). Seeing a man lying comfortable in his affliction, Jesus challenges him, "Do you want to be made well?" (John 5:6). To Martha, annoyed that her sister Mary is listening to Jesus while she makes all the meal preparations, he says, "You are worried and distracted by many things; . . . Mary has chosen the better part"(Luke 10:41–42). To his own disciples, bickering over who would be greatest in the kingdom of heaven, he says, "Whoever wants to be first among you must be last of all and servant of all." When they are panic-stricken on stormy waters, he challenges them: "Why are you afraid? Have you still no faith?" (Mark 4:40).

Jesus was so offensive to political and religious authorities because he used soft words with those the powerful regarded as expendable members of society, whom they thought he should have been rebuking, and he rebuked the power brokers of society whom they thought he should have been placating. The wise use of the gift of language can be a dangerous risk.

Many groups historically have been taught, in effect, that Proverbs 15:1 is the only language strategy available to them. They have been taught to speak when spoken to, and then only and always with a soft answer. "One who bows is not slapped," says the Korean proverb.[4] Former slave Cornelius Garner noted about the preaching his people were allowed to hear by overseers and masters: "The preaching we got wasn't anything much. The old white preacher just was telling us slaves to be good to our masters."[5]

Rosa Parks was a soft-spoken, easygoing forty-two-year-old woman who her neighbors said "would do anything for you." She found the law requiring blacks to surrender their seats to whites on buses so repugnant that she often walked the mile to and from her job as a department store seamstress. The afternoon of December 1, 1955, she boarded the Cleveland Avenue bus and, when the bus driver ordered her to get up and give her seat to a white man, instead of uttering a soft answer, "Oh, all right," she shook her head, said, "No," and continued sitting there.

Mrs. Parks, taught by her grandfather to never look on herself as inferior, and being active in the NAACP, made a split-second decision. "My feet were not tired, but I was tired—tired of unfair treatment. I stayed in my seat and slid closer to the window. I do not remember being frightened. . . . The more we gave in, the worse they treated us. I kept thinking about my mother and my grandparents, how strong they were. . . . I was just tired of giving in." She launched a 381-day boycott of the Montgomery, Alabama, bus system by black residents led by the Rev. Martin Luther King, Jr., a local minister, which forced the city to integrate its buses.[6]

Rosa Parks is not just part of history. She is shaping today's youth for the future and giving talks and workshops at high schools around the nation. She has written an autobiography called *Quiet Strength*. When asked how she would like to be remembered, she says, "As a person who wanted to be free and wanted other people also to be free." And soft answers aren't always the path to that goal in an unjust world.

So here we sit today. The sages tell us: soft words sometimes, harsh words at others. How do we know which to choose? The sages show their wisdom by not offering us an easy formula for when to give soft answers and when to risk harsh words. They respected how complex life is. Over and over again they affirm that wisdom begins with the "fear of the Lord" (Prov. 1:7), by which they meant not trembling before God's anger but acknowledging that God is the source of all moral knowledge, the giver of the gift of wisdom, the one to whom we turn when our limited understanding bumps up against the limitless complexity of daily interactions.

How else can we steer through them except by turning continually to the giver of wisdom! For most of our roles and tasks in life require both strategies: soft answers and harsh words at various times. Parenthood, friendship, marriage, relationships in the community of faith, our responsibilities as citizens, dealing with difficult people, to name just a few: these all require both language strategies and the wisdom to know when which is called for.

When Cantor Michael Weisser and his wife, Julie, moved into their new home in Lincoln, Nebraska, they had no idea that the ring of their new telephone would signal a situation that would require of them both soft answers and harsh words, and the wisdom to know when to use each. As the phone rang, Michael left the box he was unpacking to answer it. "Hello, Weisser's residence." The caller's voice said, "You will be sorry you ever moved into 5810 Randolph Street, Jew boy." Two days later the Weissers found a packet flung onto their front porch. Inside were pictures of Adolf Hitler, caricatures of Jews with hooked noses, blacks with gorilla heads, and graphic depictions of dead blacks and Jews.

It was the work of Larry Trapp, a forty-four-year-old loner who was confined to a wheelchair because of late-stage diabetes. Larry was a Nazi sympathizer and grand dragon of the KKK, responsible for terrorizing local African-American, Asian, and Jewish families. Police knew he made explosives. They didn't know he planned to blow up the Weissers' synagogue. He didn't because, despite their fear and revulsion, the Weissers reached out to Trapp, with wisely chosen alternating strategies of both harsh words and soft answers, showing him—through both—more love than he had known in his abused and abusive life.

Trapp's threatening phone calls continued. So Michael Weisser began calling Trapp. Trapp wouldn't answer, so Weisser left messages on his answering machine. "Larry," he said, "do you know that the very first laws that Hitler's Nazis passed were against people like yourself who had no legs or who had physical deformities or physical handicaps? Do you realize you would have been among the first to die under Hitler? Why do you love the Nazis so much?"

In return Larry left angry taped messages denouncing blacks, homosexuals, and Jews. Each time Weisser replied with a stern message of his own. "Justice is for everybody, Larry. . . . What are you going to say to God on your judgment day?" Meanwhile the cantor led his congregation in prayers for the grand dragon.

Then one day when Michael Weisser called, Trapp himself picked up the phone. "What do you want?" he shouted angrily. "Well," said Weisser, "I was thinking you might need a hand with something, and I wondered if I could take you to the grocery store or something." There was silence on the line. Weisser heard Trapp clear his throat and say, "That's nice of you, but I've got that covered. Thanks anyway." In subsequent phone calls, Trapp told Weisser he was "rethinking a few things." Weisser saw Trapp a few days later on TV, shrieking about the "Jew media." Furious, he picked up the phone. "This is the rabbi," he said. "It's clear you are not rethinking anything at all. I demand an explanation for what you are saying!" In a surprisingly tremulous voice, Trapp said, "I'm sorry I did that. I've been talking like that all of my life. . . . I can't help it. . . . I'll apologize."

So went the compassionate composite of language strategies by which the Weissers forged a relationship with Trapp that went far beyond words. It was one that eventually led to their taking him into their home the last nine months of his life, setting up his hospital bed in the midst of their already busy household, caring for his physical needs on days when he was kindly and days when he was irascible, nurturing his spirit while his body declined. So moved was Trapp by the Weissers' compassion that the former Grand Dragon converted to Judaism three months before he died in September 1992.[7]

Thanks to Wisdom, we know that compassion is a composite of soft answers and courageous confrontation. Thanks to Wisdom, we know there is a time to smooth the troubled waters with a soft answer and that there is a time to risk stirring up smooth waters with a harsh word. Thanks be to God who promises us, in all the tangled and tumultuous encounters that await us, the Wisdom to utter wise words.

<h2 style="text-align:center">Sermon Model C—"The Double Take"</h2>

The "Double Take" model is suited to preaching those proverbs which sound too good to be true, which present an assurance about God's protection and prospering of the righteous that, on the surface at least, is denied by our observation and experience of life. The title of this model implies that one must look again, to verify what is really being said and to evaluate whether the proverb's message can be affirmed at a level of meaning deeper than the surface. This model counteracts the caricature of Proverbs as a naive and simplistic depiction of good behavior leading to good fortune. While the Proverbs collection displays a strong element of this principle of order, at the same time it acknowledges that human attempts to order life must contend with the limitations of human knowledge, the mystery of God's plans, and the dangers of making wrong choices and falling prey to the plans of evil, greedy fools. This model honors the collection's affirmation that, while these dangers and uncertainties lurk in life, still wisdom is its own reward, one far more valuable than economic prosperity (Prov. 11:8, 28). For the pursuit of wisdom brings to individuals within the community of the wise the flourishing of inward integrity (14:32; 20:7), a closeness to God (15:29), and joy (10:28).[8]

Some suggestions for proverbs that lend themselves to this model are:

Proverbs 10:2, 3, 24, 28
       11: 8, 17, 18, 19, 21, 23, 25, 28
       12: 3, 7, 13, 21, 28
       13: 3, 6, 9, 14, 18, 21
       14:14, 19, 26, 27, 32
       15:6, 19, 25, 29

16: 3, 17
18:10
19:16, 23
20:7
21:21
22:4
24:19–20
28:14, 18, 19, 26
30:5

This sermon model allows the meaning of biblical proverbs that create order to be deepened by those which subvert that order, affirming that human knowledge is limited, that life is unpredictable, but that our sovereign God, while to a degree inscrutable, is faithful in the face of both the unfair and the unknown.

SERMON:
The Highway of the Upright Avoids Evil:
"Too Good to Be True?"

> *Text:* "The highway of the upright avoids evil; those who guard their way preserve their lives." (Prov. 16:17)
>
> *Context:* Graduate Recognition Sunday

I am always in the process of reading a novel, because novels give the gift of new insights about real life. A few evenings ago I read the scene from a novel written by Alice Hoffman in the late 1980s, in which Polly takes the thermometer out of her daughter Amanda's mouth, and stands next to her bed reading it and trying not to look as worried as she feels. "You'll be better in the morning," Polly says. It's what she always says when the children are sick, and they always believe her. But this time Polly is wrong. In the morning, the last day of August and hottest on record, Amanda will still be shivering beneath two cotton quilts.

Amanda is an eleven-year-old girl who contracts a disease, AIDS, that no one ever thought would touch the small New England town where her family lives. We adults, like Polly, consider it our job to assure children that everything will be all right, especially today, Graduate Recognition Sunday. For today we celebrate their accomplishments and wish them well as they move on to new jobs or schools. Still, while smooth reassurances are flowing from our lips, a part of us is haunted by the truth embodied in the title Alice Hoffman gives her novel about Polly and Amanda and the community around them: *At Risk.*

At the same time that I have been reading *At Risk,* I have been reading devotionally through the book of Proverbs. The same night that I read the excerpt from *At Risk,* I read chapter 16, verse 17: "The highway of the upright avoids evil; those who guard their way preserve their lives." I thought to myself, Could this proverb mean what it sounds as if it does—that nothing bad will ever happen to those who seek God?

Normally my devotional reading quiets my mind for sleep, but this time I fell into a restless sleep, my mind still working through this troubling prospect.

Scenes and faces floated before me.

Here is the young couple who, on their way home from an alcohol-free prom, were hit and killed by a drunk driver.

Here is the biblical character Job sitting by the road, covered in festering boils, the graves of his children before his eyes, his friends turning on him.

Here is a mass grave yawning in the earth in the town that was one of the so-called "protected areas" of Bosnia-Herzegovina.

I awoke with a headache, the words of the proverb pounding in my temples: "The highway of the upright avoids evil; those who guard their way preserve their lives." If this means that no evil, no tragedy will befall those who trust in God, then the person who wrote this must have been dreaming—or living in a different world from our own!

If the proverb means that when we trust in God we are no longer *at risk* in this life, then it makes a false promise and I should skip over this verse.

But this proverb is not making so vast a claim. The proverb isn't making a blanket, bogus promise that nothing bad will ever happen to those who seek God. The word the NRSV translates as *avoids* means "turns aside from," picturing the individual on the highway of the righteous actively making choices to avoid evil. The proverb is pointing out that wise choices we make every day can guard us from some of life's evil and keep us on a safe, secure path.

Once in the mountains of Colorado our family was driving up a steep, winding road. We were so far above sea level that our ears were popping, our heads getting light. Suddenly one of the children shrieked, "Daddy, look, there's no guardrail!" This was something both of us parents had already noticed, but we were hoping the children hadn't. Now, of course, everybody in the car looked over to the right, to the place where a guardrail was desperately needed and conspicuously absent—because there was not enough level ground to put one. "There's nothing to shriek about," we reassured the children. "Just keep your eyes on the road, and we'll get you up the mountain."

What parents today aren't haunted by the sense that they are traveling with their children along a steep and dangerous path with no guardrail? We keep hoping our children don't notice. What parents don't pray that if their children just stay on the wise path they've shown them by teaching and example, they'll be all right? What parents don't say that to their children, praying that it is true?

The week before my oldest daughter left home to go to college, I was washing dishes in the kitchen and she was packing her things in her basement room. The sounds of Cat Stevens's lyrics wafted up the stairs: "Oh baby baby it's a wild world, it's hard to get by just upon a smile. You know I've seen a lot of what the world can do, and it's breaking my heart in two, 'cause I never want to see you sad girl, . . . but if you want to leave take good care, hope you make a lot of nice friends out there, but just remember there's a lot of bad and beware. Oh, baby, baby, it's a wild world."[9]

"Oh, shut up, Cat!" I said to the empty kitchen. "She's not listening to your lyrics, and there's nothing I can do about them!"

When I read Proverbs I realize I am not the first to suffer the symptoms of parental anxiety at those forces that put our children's lives at risk. Proverbs were used by fathers and mothers in Israelite homes to instruct the young in the kinds of practices that endanger and those that protect their life. Israelite parents told their young that Wisdom provided guidance for their path and a degree of protection for their life. There are two words for life in the Proverbs collection: *ḥayyim* and *nepeš*. *Ḥayyim* defines life as good health, good name, a degree of prosperity, and long years. *Nepeš* is used in this proverb and refers to the inward breathing, feeling, thinking person who both affects and is affected by the circumstances of life. "Those who guard their way preserve their lives."

Avoiding evil, the proverb claims, protects that inward life from harm. What kind of evil, in particular? Malicious speech, for one thing. We teach our children, "Honesty is the best policy," and "Mud thrown is ground lost."

Parental sages through the ages have warned their young against the evils of bad company. We teach our preschoolers never to follow a stranger off the beaten path into the woods to look for a lost puppy. We send our young elementary children to Drug and Alcohol Resistance Education Programs (DARE). "Just say no," we tell them. "A person is known by the company she keeps."

Dr. J. J. Starks, who a generation ago served as president of two black colleges in South Carolina—Morris and Benedict—listed six things that destroy students: "Bad company, keeping late hours, gaming as a pastime, disregard for values, failure to discriminate between love and lust, and the drink habit."[10] Add crack, heroin, and inhalants, and, to us adults, that still seems like a sound "don't do" list.

"The highway of the upright avoids evil; those who guard their way preserve their lives." That would make a pretty good exit line as we wave goodbye to our young adults who are graduating today.

But suppose as we walk away the young adult we've just quoted this proverb to comes running after us, grabs us by the sleeve, and challenges our parting proverb. "Wait a minute, Dad, Mom, Grandma, Uncle Bill—I have a friend who has AIDS. I have a friend whose little sister was killed in a drive-by shooting. I know people who can't find jobs after years of training. Even if I guard my path and turn aside from evil speech and habits and people, tragedy can leap the guardrail and loom in the middle of my path. What do I do then?"

We can picture the sages of Israel standing by the railway platform or in the dorm corridor, nodding in appreciation of what a great question this is! Do you ever fear that as parents in our homes and as adult role models in the church we have placed more emphasis on the "don't dos" of avoiding trouble than on the "what to dos" for the time it strikes?

What do I do then? our youth want to know. The sages, amid all their assurances that wisdom preserves life from evil, had thought of this question too. These same sages who taught the young to plan life to avoid evil knew that anything can happen and probably will. "Do not boast about tomorrow, for you do not know what a day may bring" (27:1).

The sages knew that life contains an unpredictable zone, and it is precisely in this zone that God is encountered.

When our path veers into a zone of illness, tragedy, injustice, what does Proverbs recommend that we do, youth and adults alike? The book of Proverbs doesn't recommend isolating oneself and crying, "Why me?" or bitterly blaming God. Instead we are to seek the company and support of other seekers of wisdom. Walking together along life's twisting path, we are to seek a God who, though to a degree shrouded in mystery, is a constant giver of Wisdom's presence to nourish our inward lives, even when our path is overcome by danger and tragedy.

"The highway of the upright avoids evil; those who guard their way preserve their lives." Think back over those occasions in the past few years when evil has refused to avoid our path. Have we modeled a community of people who guard our way from bitterness and isolation? Have we preserved our lives together by seeking the gift of divine Wisdom, praying for faith in the face of mystery, gathering as a community of wisdom seekers to support and guide one another when the highway of the upright twists and turns?

A young woman named Vivian Johnson writes of her great love for her younger brother. "He's my little brother. At least that's what I called him until he grew a foot taller than I. If a sister wants her brother as a source of pride, my brother fits the ticket. All the external trophies are there: successful business executive, responsible church member, supporter of the arts, meticulous dresser, plus a glistening apartment with a view. More importantly, the internal characteristics are also present. He is a person of deep Christian commitment, full of compassion, and generous in spirit, as well as with his resources. John is a keeper.

"I wasn't prepared for the bad news. 'Vivian, I have something important to tell you,' my brother said while he and I were seated at my kitchen table. His eyes centered on mine as he reached out and touched my hand. His voice became thin and tight: 'I want you to know I've been diagnosed as HIV-positive.' . . . No! my brain shouted. Tears threatened from somewhere deep in my throat. Before I could respond, he assured me, 'Spiritually I am healthy. I depend on God for strength and on my church for support. I would appreciate your prayers, Vivian'."[11]

Holding onto God's presence and turning to the church and the prayers of friends and family, John is guarding his way and, at the deepest level, trusting God to preserve his life.

A clergy colleague of mine tells of an experience with a parishioner we'll call Robin. Robin was a very achievement-oriented woman in her mid-thirties, a borderline control freak who believed in planning every detail of her life. She balked when any aspect of life did not follow the plan. Whenever something went less than perfectly at church, Robin would be the first to get on the phone and inform the pastor. Comments she had made in Sunday school class and casual conversation told my pastor friend that she was a reluctant church member, there largely to please her husband and keep peace in the home. Both God and the church were on probation with Robin. She was checking them out, seeing what benefit they could be to her life.

My friend was away at a conference when it happened. Gary, Robin's husband, whose health had always seemed good, had had an unexplained seizure and been rushed to the hospital in the middle of the night. His doctors were not sure what the problem was and were running every imaginable test to determine the cause of the seizure.

My friend walked the long hospital hall to Gary's room, preparing for her encounter with Robin, rehearsing all the defenses of God she could remember from theology classes in seminary. She knew that Robin truly needed God now, but that she would be so severely put out by this unexpected interruption in life's schedule that she might descend into bitterness. Rounding the final corner, she came face to face with Robin. She braced herself, but Robin's face had lost its usual sober expression and was wearing a rare smile of welcome for her pastor.

"Hello, pastor!" Robin said warmly. "I have to tell you that I never knew until this crisis what Christian community really meant. People we don't even know that well, people we have never done any favors for, have sent us cards, have called us to tell us we're in their prayers, have offered to make meals for us. Gary and I don't know what the outcome of all this will be, but we have never felt God's presence more closely than we have in the support of the church these past few days."

God and God's community were with Robin and Gary on this bleak stretch of life's path. Have we adults taught and modeled for our graduates that when our highway turns into tragedy, we can risk putting our lives in the hands of our faithful yet mysterious God, in whose presence we can withstand the worst life has to dole out? Have we taught them and shown them this God who guards our way and, at the deepest level of our experience, preserves our lives, whatever losses we may encounter?

"The highway of the upright avoids evil"? Not necessarily. But can we guard our way by turning our inward lives toward the gift of divine Wisdom's presence? Always, thanks be to God!

9

Set for the
Rise and Fall of Many:
Preaching Proverbs That
Subvert Order

The central dynamic of this model is based on the rhetorical strategy of placing two proverbs that offer contrasting interpretations side by side in relation to a particular situation. This dynamic occurs in Proverbs itself (26:4, 5). Within the collection as a whole there are proverbs that trace poverty to laziness (10:4; 12:11; 19:15; 20:4; 20:13; 21:17; 23:20–21), and there are those which counsel respect for the poor as the will of God (14:21, 31; 15:25; 17:5; 19:17; 21:13; 22:9, 22, 23; 28:27; 29:14). There are proverbs that praise nonconfrontative speech (15:1) as well as many that laud the positive effects of rebuke (10:17; 12:1; 13:1; 15:10, 12, 31, 32; 25:12; 28:23). There are opposing proverbs concerning the results of proverb use itself (15:23; 25:11 and 26:7, 9).

Qohelet's use of proverbs often is to juxtapose two sayings, the first expressing a precept of traditional wisdom, and the second, probably of his own coinage, subverting the first. "Dueling Proverbs" is often the strategy of choice of the prophets. By this strategy, God via the prophet quotes a current proverb or saying that encapsulates the common human interpretation of the situation, then overturns it with a diametrically opposed saying encapsulating the divine will for the situation (Isa. 49:14, 15; Ezek. 12:21–23; 18:1–4; 18:25–29; 33:10–11; 37:11–14).

Jesus often quotes an existing proverb, then quotes or coins another one to subvert it. "An eye for an eye and a tooth for a tooth. . . . If anyone strikes you on the right cheek, turn the other also" (Matt. 5:38–39). "Doctor, cure yourself. . . . No prophet is accepted in the prophet's hometown" (Luke 4:23–24).

When preaching a "dueling proverbs" sermon, the cultural proverb is brought in first, with the preacher suggesting situations from daily life in which we often hear this proverb quoted. Then the biblical proverb is brought in, which subverts the cultural proverb and offers a radically different interpretation of these and other situations. A few suggestions to spark further reflection are:

"You are what you eat." "It is not what goes into the mouth that defiles a person, but it is what comes out of the mouth that defiles" (Matt. 15:11; Mark 7:15).

"Every person has his price." "For what will it profit them if they gain the whole world but forfeit their life?" (Matt. 16:26; Mark 8:36; Luke 9:25).

"If you've got it, flaunt it." "No one after lighting a lamp puts it under the bushel basket, but on the lampstand, and it gives light to all in the house" (Matt. 5:15; Mark 4:21; Luke 8:16).

"Don't get mad, get even." "If anyone strikes you on the right cheek, turn the other also" (Matt. 5:39; Luke 6:29).

It is also possible to allow a subversive proverb from the New Testament to duel with an order proverb from the Hebrew Bible. For example, "The reward for humility and fear of the Lord is riches and honor and life" (Prov. 22:4) could be faced with "Those who want to save their life will lose it, and those who lose their life for my sake will save it" (Luke 9:24 and parallels).[1]

Sermon:
Those Who Want to Save Their Life Will Lose It:
"Finders Weepers, Losers Keepers"

Text: "For those who want to save their life will lose it, and those who lose their life for my sake will find it." (Matt. 16:25)

In the entryway of our church sits a large brown box. The box is large, but it must not be large enough, because it is always overflowing. The box is pushed under an old pew next to a wall, its contents always spilling out into the hallway, almost tripping passersby.

The box is our church's lost-and-found box.

One Sunday morning, several minutes before the eleven-o'clock service was to begin, I knelt beside the box, rooting through it, looking for my son's missing blue mitten. I didn't find the mitten, but I did find a house key on a key chain shaped like a sneaker. I found a man's red neck scarf. I found a child's well-worn nap blanket. I found a pair of reading glasses.

I was surprised to find these necessary items left unclaimed. I felt an urgent need to pick up the overflowing box and take it into church with me, walking up and down the aisles, holding up first one necessary item and then the next: searching for the man with the cold neck, the woman squinting at an upside-down bulletin, the teenager locked out of his house, the child crying for her blanket. How could the lost-and-found box at my church be filled with such crucial items, sitting unclaimed and forgotten?

There was one other thing I found in that box, at the very bottom, all covered in dust. It was a saying of Jesus, "Those who want to save their life will lose it, and those who lose their life for my sake will find it." That is a proverb. It was dark in the entryway, and the words glowed as I brushed off the dust. Like a flashlight or a spotlight—that's what a proverb is, a spotlight meant to illuminate certain situations in life, but not all of them. "Like somebody who takes a passing dog by the ears is one who meddles in the quarrel of another" (Prov. 26:17) was a proverb that suggested a wise course to me recently when I was contemplating stepping in and mediating a quarrel that two friends of mine were having. But this proverb would not be an appropriate send-off to a Secretary of State sent by her country to mediate a dispute between nations. Proverbs illuminate some situations for some people, but not every situation for all people.

Jesus often spoke in proverbs. Sometimes he borrowed proverbs already in use around him. Like, "Doctor, cure yourself." "If a blind person leads a blind person, they'll both fall into a pit."

Sometimes Jesus coined new proverbs, known as aphorisms, which overturned normative practices and wisdom of his day. "The sabbath was made for humankind, not humankind for the sabbath." "There is nothing outside a person that by going in can defile, but the things that come out are what defile." One of Jesus' most memorable proverbs expresses criticism of the superficial, self-preserving existence that many called life in his day, as in our own, "If any want to become my followers, let them deny themselves and take up their cross and follow me. For those who want to save their life will lose it, and those who lose their life for my sake will save it."

Like all proverbs, this one is appropriate for some situations, but not for all situations. When misused, any proverbs, especially this one, can obscure as well as illumine, hurt as well as help. Just think how this proverb has been misused in the history of the church. When mistaken for a universal truth it implies that any time we suffer, experience loss or death, God heaves a sigh of satisfaction.

It's been quoted, as in the early church, as a blanket endorsement of martyrdom. "Get into that arena; never mind the lion's growl."

It's been quoted by masters to slaves to deceive them into thinking they are really quite fortunate to be slowly dying in the fields.

It's been quoted by pastors to women in abusive situations. "There's a cross for everyone and there's a cross for you. The husband is the head of the wife. Be comforted by the words of our Savior, 'If anyone would save her life, she must lose it, and whoever loses her life for Jesus' sake, will find it.'"

By this use, I should walk up and down the aisles of my church, your church, any and every church, carrying the lost-and-found box, hocking this proverb as the antidote to everybody's involuntary suffering. "If anyone would save his life he will lose it; whoever loses her life for my sake and the gospel's will find it." Where is the widower whose bereavement has stretched into long days in front of the talk shows and evenings with the sitcoms and a bottle? Where is the overworked, underappreciated employee? Where is the young adult who has tremendous acting ability, but whose parents will only pay for an accounting degree? This implies that God likes it best when we're suffering. It is as if God is only pleased when we're sacrificing, it doesn't matter what or why, just sacrificing. As if, in God's eyes, only when we are helpless, then are we righteous. Better to leave the proverb in the lost-and-found box than to take it out and use it to hurt and mislead!

Friends of mine have two girls, six and four, and were expecting a third child, which they knew was going to be a boy. At the crucial three-month mark, they suffered a miscarriage. We had the two girls over for supper and a sleep-over while their parents were at the hospital. In the middle of the meatloaf, six-year old Emily looked up and informed us in that matter-of-fact way children have, "We were going to have a baby brother, but now we're not. My mommy says there are a lot of different ways to die."

I murmured some comforting words, but inside I was saying, "You can say that again, Emily!" In just the past few days a teenage boy had been beaten severely by other teens and left to die on the steps of a church where he had been an altar boy, and four children had died in a house fire caused by careless smoking . . .

Jesus couldn't walk two steps without being reminded of the different ways there were to die in his day. The Romans often nailed two innocent pieces of wood together and used them to inflict brutal and excruciating deaths. In the past several chapters that precede our text from Matthew, Jesus has met a lot of living deaths: two men tortured by inward demons, a leper, two blind men, a woman watching her daughter suffer torments, a crowd of starving people. And not once has he quoted this aphorism to them: "For those who want to save their life will lose it, and those who lose their life for my sake will find it," and walked on by! Instead, he has exorcised, healed, and fed.

The proverb is not simply a palliative for all those situations in which we or others are suffering unjustly or painfully. It's not so we can tell ourselves and others: "Accept the pain, accept the abuse, accept the injustice. That's your cross." As if crosses, cruel, unjust, death-dealing crosses are automatically good things, somehow. Social ethicist Beverly Wildung Harrison, in her essay "The Power of Anger in the Work of Love," pinpoints the heresy that happens when we "rip the crucifixion of Jesus out of its lived-world context in his total life and historical project and turn sacrifice into an abstract norm for the Christian life. . . . To be sure, Jesus was faithful unto death. He stayed with his cause and he died for it as he had lived for it. He *accepted* sacrifice. But his sacrifice was *for* the cause of radical love, to right wrong relationship, which is what we call 'doing justice.'"[2]

The cross is not about making a virtue out of other people's brutal suffering and abuse. No, when Jesus says to take up our cross he means, "Voluntarily seek out, embrace opportunities to alleviate involuntary, unjust suffering—of others, your own." A cross is a voluntary exchange of our definition of life with Jesus' view of life in God's present and coming kingdom. We've all heard the contemporary proverb "Finders keepers, losers weepers." Jesus' proverb reverses it. "Finders weepers, losers keepers."

We're brought up to be finders: striving to find life defined as prosperity, hard work, long life, health, orderly affairs, others' thinking well of us, avoiding persons who would jeopardize our comfortable way of life.

Jesus challenges us to become carefree losers, losing that superficial, self-absorbed view of life! In that challenge is the promise that we will find life built around a different preoccupation: with God's present and coming kingdom. Become losers of anxiety about the orderly life, the opinions of powerful others. Become keepers, collectors, of radical acts of love for others, acts that lead to justice, acts that can be subversive and costly in their results, but which lead to life. Not martyrs, but rather seekers of love.

John Dominic Crossan calls this losing/saving paradox "frightening good news." We have to lose something we want to hold onto, to gain something we don't yet fully understand. It whispers to us that "we should fear what we have always wanted and do what we have always feared."[3]

Jesus in our passage uses this proverb to spotlight the coming event of his own death, not because pain and humiliation and untimely death are abstract virtues God wants us all to seek, but because he had discovered that life was to be found in a preoccupation with radical love for others, and let the chips fall where they may. So central is this understanding to his identity that Matthew places it right before the Transfiguration.

God would not allow such a life to be lost. Rather, the resurrection proves that losers are keepers, as Jesus' restored and expanded presence lives in our midst in the Spirit today. I sense the wisdom of the risen Christ whispering that the proverb is not for Emily's parents, in some enforced affirmation of the loss of their child. It is for the rest of the neighborhood to give up their fear of tragedy and their self-absorption and become alive with empathy in deeds of listening and love and meals and visits and prayers and cards to a family suffering a loss. This proverb is not for the teenager who lies dying, his skull fractured on the church steps. The proverb is for that church—all churches—to lose their "it couldn't happen here" complex and become alive in ministry to his parents and family and to other teens and their families in the wake of violent outbursts.

As I kneel over the lost-and-found box, brushing the dust off this proverb, I feel the wisdom of the risen Christ, saying to us, "There are a lot of different ways to live!" To whom is Christ the Wisdom of God urging me and you to offer this life-giving, light-giving proverb today, as we walk up and down the aisles of our churches, lost-and-found box in hand?

Offer it to the suburbs being challenged by cities to view the problems of drugs, poverty, poor schools, and violence as common problems, rather than as threats from which to hide, to see them as opportunities to give of their influence and resources. Losers, keepers.

Offer it to the mainline churches of this country squinting over attendance graphs, asking peevishly, "Why are these boomers so self-centered? Why are these slackers so slack?" "Why can't they be like we were, perfect in every way? What's the matter with folks today?" They need to be challenged to give up a preoccupation with institutional survival for a risky attempt to interpret theological jargon in terms that matter to people today. To sing, worship, and preach in modes that, without compromising the gospel, are compelling to those to whom it is addressed in this age. Losers keepers.

When, guided by the wisdom and power of Wisdom-in-person, Jesus the Crucified and Risen Sage, we accept for ourselves and offer to others the gift of this crucial, unclaimed proverb, we find that now the church's lost-and-found box is empty. But let's find another use for it—let's recycle the lost-and-found box. Like the prophets imagining hopeful visions of the end-time, like the seers transported over the earth in dreamlike visions, sometimes I let my mind range back through history, hovering over the earth of Jesus' day, searching for all the instruments of all the "different ways to die." You come with me. Let's grasp the swords from their place on the soldiers' hips, let's pick up the thrown stones from the ground, let's close our hands around every torturous cross, from every groaning hill. Into the box with them! Then let's come forward in time to the present and range over the earth looking for today's instruments of death. Let's not stop until we have visited every police station, every dumpster, every gun shop, every church steps. Where is the Super Slugger bat? Throw it in the box! Where are the empty Jack Daniels bottles, the syringes? Throw them in! Where are the assault weapons? Throw them in!

Then let's walk up and down the aisles of your church, my church, any church holding the box, looking for chains that have bound people to a safety that no longer satisfies—and throw them in! Looking for false crosses of abuse too long accepted, too long inflicted—throw them in!

Let's pray that one day we can rename our lost-and-found box the lost box. Because it will contain all the instruments of death that, by the power of God who sent and raised Jesus Christ, will one day be lost forever, and never missed for a moment. Because we'll all be too preoccupied with using what once lay at the bottom of the box, our lost-and-found proverb. Our thoughts will be preoccupied with all the many ways there are to live in this world, by the power and Wisdom of God in Christ. Humankind will have its mind on lighting up our world one situation at a time.

SERMON MODEL E—"THE CHALLENGER"

This model allows a subversive proverb to challenge both church and culture. It calls the church to be true to its own best wisdom and does not allow it to take refuge in condemnations of "the world" that divert it from its own shortcomings. The preacher as sage lifts up a subversive biblical proverb from the Hebrew Scriptures or the New Testament (or some combination of the two) and asks, How does this proverb(s) criticize both communities of faith and cultural mores for furthering practices and systems that keep people isolated and miserable?

A sermon could be preached challenging abuses of hierarchical power in church and culture based on Mark 10:43–44 ("Whoever wishes to become great among you must be your servant, and whoever wishes to be first among you must be slave of all") in the context of the whole of chapter 10. A challenge to the secular gospel of success and prosperity could be issued by a saying from Qohelet that challenges conventional wisdom's promises to bring long life, health, and reputation in light of the inequities and limitations of life (1:18), paired with a New Testament text that offers a positive account of how Christian wisdom helps us deal with these realities. (1 Cor. 1:18–31; Rom. 5:1–5) Workaholism and the acquisitiveness that often motivates it could be challenged by one of Qohelet's repeated questionings of the value of toil (3:9; 4:4; 6:7), in conjunction with Jesus' aphorism "Consider the lilies of the field, how they grow" (Matt. 6:28) or Paul's affirmations of salvation apart from works.

A few possibilities from the Hebrew Scriptures include Eccl. 7:2; Prov. 19:21; 21:30.

The challenger sermon focuses on situations in the life of the faith community as well as the culture that stand in need of the word of subversive critique implied in the biblical proverb. It then moves to projecting the visions of redeemed situations in the life of church and culture that happen when worshipers take it seriously, by the power of God's grace.

The "Challenger" sermon can highlight a subversive biblical proverb that has been used by dominant groups to suppress others and replace the oppressive interpretation with a subversive one. For example, "Those who want to save their life will lose it, and those who lose their life for my sake, and for the sake of the gospel will save it" (Mark 8:35 and parallels).

SERMON:
Better Off Is the One Who Has Not Yet Been: "The Fortunate Ones"

> *Texts:* "Better off than both the living and the dead are those who have not been born." (Eccl. 4:3)
>
> "Then he withdrew from them about a stone's throw, knelt down, and prayed." (Luke 22:41)
>
> "In his anguish he prayed more earnestly, and his sweat became like great drops of blood falling down on the ground." (Luke 22:44)
>
> *Context:* Advent

When I was a child of five or six, our family attended a church that had on the back wall a massive stained-glass window divided into two panels. I spent each Sunday chin on my hands on top of the pew, facing the back, looking at first one half of the window, then the other, then back again. The panel on the right pictured a man kneeling against a rock, his hands locked in prayer, his eyes turned toward heaven, an anguished expression on his face. Each week I would stare at that poor man, wondering why he was so unhappy and what he was praying for. Tears dotted his checks, and on sunny Sundays they would glisten as the sun filtered through the window.

I would count each shining droplet and then I would switch my eyes to the panel on the left. This picture was of what looked like the same man; his features were identical. But it couldn't be, because his posture and attitude seemed so different. This man was standing upright, his level gaze looking straight at me, a serene and confident look in his eye. No tears on this side of the window. His hands were not interlocked in anguished beseeching but stretched serenely at his sides, open-palmed, as if to receive the power of God to lift him in the direction he appeared to be going, which was up. Every week I would pray to the serene man, beseeching him to glance across the window to the man on the other side—"Look over there at that man crying, with no one to comfort him. Can't you do something to help him?"

Many years have passed since I was six. I like to think that I am still very sensitive to the tears of others. I watch the news nightly. I read the paper daily. In fact, I do both at the same time, with the remote control on the couch beside me, to mute the commercials so I can read the paper until the news comes back on. Last week I had just watched an in-depth story about the rising incidence of asthma among inner-city children. I muted the commercial showing smiling children in the latest holiday fashions from a local department store so I could read an article about the number of children killed in house fires in a nearby city. Glancing up, I saw that the news had come back on with the sound still muted. I saw a full-screen picture of a young girl's face. She was a first- or second-grader with a gap-toothed smile. Then, one after the other, there came the image of a junkyard, a car, a river, and a relief worker pulling a small bundle out of the river. Still I didn't push the button to get the soundtrack back. I already knew the soundtrack, just as surely as Qohelet, the wise teacher who taught in Palestine in the fifth century before the birth of Jesus, knew the soundtrack to the tragic scenes of injustice he witnessed in his day. The little girl had played in the junkyard, lived in the car, and died in the river. If Qohelet were the announcer instead of Tom Brokaw, his commentary would be, "Look, the tears of the oppressed, with no one to comfort them!"

Then a commercial began, with images of a beaming brother and sister in matching red sleepers discovering their presents under a gleaming tree. Suddenly the sound blared on again, as my six-year-old son grabbed the remote from my hand. He had been watching the screen from behind the couch, waiting for the chance to pop out and scare me. He grinned his gap-toothed smile at me, and then his expression became more serious as he pointed toward the screen and offered his commentary: "I feel sorry for the children on the real news. The children on the commercials are much happier."

In the days leading up to Christmas, it is as if there were a two-part stained-glass window glowing before our eyes. On the one side is the ideal Christmas. It depicts a family tableau, a happy group clustered around a tree, the sun lighting up their red and green velvet holiday clothing, glinting on the richly patterned wrapping paper, glittering through the ribbons, making the apples and pears on the festive platter glow deep maroon and yellow, the lights on the tree sparkle. Closing our eyes, we can hear the sounds of "There's No Place like Home for the Holidays." We can smell the scent of pine, the aroma of sugar cookies about to be taken out of the oven.

This ideal Christmas is the kind you enjoy if you're really fortunate—in material terms and in terms of having loving, rich relationships with others. This is the kind of Christmas, if you are less fortunate in material or relational terms, you wish you were going to enjoy. This is the kind of scene Qohelet would have urged his students to enjoy to the hilt as a gift from God. He believed that because life is inequitable and often tragic, we should look for and accept the gift of enjoyment in our particular corner of life, which he called our portion, whenever it presented itself. Enjoy your family. Enjoy your work. Enjoy your meal. For the possibility of enjoyment of our portion in life is a gift from God (Eccl. 5:18–20).

Qohelet would point us to the many sounds, sights, events, and feelings there are to enjoy this season: school concerts, delicious food, parties, more delicious food, music wherever you go, beautiful lights lighting up the neighborhood, family gatherings where loving fellowship is possible, gifts wrapped in beautiful ribbons. So as we feast our eyes on the ideal Christmas side of the window, Qohelet would say, "Enjoy! However limited your portion is, whatever uncertainties today holds, enjoy it and say thank you to God."

There is another side to the two-part Advent window we are imagining. There are those who look forward to a less than ideal Christmas, those society calls the less fortunate, those who are homeless, those who are bereaved or abused, the children who peruse the Toys R Us catalog that came in the mail, marking the items they want Santa to bring them, while their parents look on hopelessly. There are those who have trouble following Qohelet's advice to find joy in their present portion. The depictions of the ideal Christmas that fill every billboard and television screen only make their misery more obvious to them and the world.

Ironically, Advent in this culture is a season that deepens the divide between the fortunates and the less fortunates, the haves and the have-nots, the powerful and the powerless, the ideal and the real. There is a temptation for both sides of the window, the fortunate and the less fortunate. Those society calls the more fortunate, those who have warm family relationships and well-decorated homes, those who can afford the presents and the tree, may be tempted to feel these are all the gifts they need this Christmas. Those who are less fortunate, who can look at the catalog but can't place any orders, who look through the window at the family feast but are alone, may feel uncomforted by the season, as if there is no gift for them this Christmas.

We would say that Qohelet belonged on the more fortunate side of society. He was, after all, a wisdom teacher who probably made a comfortable enough living. He had mixed feelings about why the less fortunate had smaller portions than the fortunate. Some of his colleagues said it was because they needed to seek wisdom more earnestly or work harder. He himself thought it was God's doing, but at the same time felt it was in part due to powerful, greedy people robbing the powerless (Eccl. 5:18). In any case, he didn't really think there was much anybody could do about life's inequities. Qohelet believed that we live in an unjust world ruled over by a mysterious God who calls us to accept the divine gift of enjoying the possibilities of one's own lot moment to moment. Given that outlook, I wonder why he left his comfortable home or school and rambled around town and countryside, observing the plight of the less fortunate.

The only explanation is compassion, empathy: he simply could not keep his gaze away from them. While he often counseled others to eat and drink and find enjoyment in their toil, the knowledge that there were those who didn't have enough to eat and drink distracted him from fully following his own advice. There is an unspoken yearning between the lines of this passage from chapter 4. "If only something could be done!" Qohelet seems to say. It was the same helpless feeling I had as a child looking at the tears of the man crying in the Garden, the same helpless feeling I have now as I read the paper and hear details I would rather not know on the evening news.

If Qohelet were walking the highways and byways of Advent this year, he would be pointing from his fortunate side of the window to the other side, saying to us, "Look—the tears of the oppressed with no one to comfort them! Enjoy your portion this Christmas, but at the same time come out with me and let me show you."

If we were to follow him, I think he would take us to those who are shedding tears out of our sight, off our beaten paths, in secret places of pain. There is a woman sewing gold lamé blouses in a sweatshop. There is a woman standing in front of a mirror, trying to cover a bruised eye with makeup. There is a man standing, head bowed, in the aisle in a department store. He has just spotted the perfect gift for his wife this Christmas, but she died this time last year. There is a man weeping in a prison cell in the dead of night. There is a young woman settling her children down for the night in their cots at the homeless shelter.

These were the kinds of scenes and people that caused Qohelet to coin a new proverb that offered a disturbing definition of who was really more fortunate and who less fortunate in society. "And I thought the dead, who have already died, more fortunate than the living, who are still alive; but better than both is the one who has not yet been, and has not seen all the evil deeds that are done under the sun" (4:2–3). If Qohelet were to craft a stained-glass window for our Advent contemplation, on the lucky side would be, not a vivid visual feast of well-clad, well-fed folk, but a blank windowpane to signify those who have not yet been born. And on the less fortunate side would be you, me, and all the living—less fortunate than the unborn because we have experience of our own and others' sufferings, knowledge of injustices meted out and received.

Qohelet's is the despair of the privileged observer of others' suffering, the sight of which has ruined forever for him the comforting worldview of traditional wisdom that life is just, and if Santa didn't bring you any gifts, it was because you weren't good. He does not offer a plan to improve the lot of the poor and abused, but rather offers a grim observation of what are, to him, life's inevitable injustices.

Still, his tears, his sleepless nights, are an early Christmas gift to us. We often hear the question at this season: "What do you give the person who has everything?" This proverb of Qohelet's would be a good choice! His proverb "Better than both the living and the dead are those who have not been born" is a poignant reminder that while both church and culture are eating, drinking, and enjoying their Advent preparations and Christmas celebrations, there are those who are wishing they had never been born. His gift is the gift of the summons to "Look, the tears of the oppressed . . . "

Answering his summons, let us train our gaze on the man I mentioned at the outset, crying in the Garden. As a child I wondered what had gotten him into such a tragic situation. Now I know. It was that he had a disturbing picture of who is more and who is less fortunate, which he painted in his wise teachings and embodied with his life. On the more fortunate side of his window were the very people we define as less fortunate: the hungry, the crying, the persecuted, the destitute, and the poor. Why the switch? Because they would be filled, would laugh, would be rewarded. On the less fortunate side of his window, he placed those we normally place on the more fortunate side: those who have plenty to eat, who are wealthy and consoled by life's material possessions, enjoying their portions undistracted by the sufferings of those in their communities. Why the switch? Because they will be hungry, and they will lose their present, shallow consolations.

"Look," said Jesus over and over again, in parable, proverb, and admonition, pointing our eyes to the future in the present: "The tears of those who have been distracted by their wealth and have ignored the plight of the poor, with none to comfort them!" Jesus shared Qohelet's compassion for the oppressed and the suffering. But he did not blame God, or view injustice as inevitable. He placed blame where it belonged, threatening the religious and political principalities and powers of his day. He bestowed the privilege of his companionship on the marginalized and destitute. And he still does. He was often rejected by those at the center of social power. And he still is. He made a choice to identify with those who were suffering. And because of that radical, lifelong identification, he suffered brutal torture and was killed.

One Sunday in church as I gazed at the window behind me, my mother, after her third attempt to get me to turn around and face forward, finally demanded, "Why do you keep looking at that window?" "I'm praying for that happy man to do something to help that sad man," I told her, pointing from one to the other. Then my mother gave proof of why she has been such an effective Sunday school teacher for second-graders for so many years. "They're both the same man," she explained. "After he prays in the Garden he is killed, but God raises him from the dead. He's still alive today praying for people who are sad and helping to comfort them."

This Advent, that means that every person and every household is fortunate, for each of our portions includes the presence of Christ. He offers us the gift of comfort in our own sufferings and his companionship as we seek to bring comfort to the sufferings of those shedding tears around us. To point to people wishing they were dead or had never been born in our community is to point to people in whose lives God is already at work bringing comfort and hope.

Steve Arrington was a navy frogman specializing in bomb disposal who had done several tours of duty rescuing downed pilots in Vietnam. Through a series of mistakes in judgment he became involved in piloting flights smuggling cocaine from Colombia to California. He became the fall guy in the John Delorean drug case, the most highly publicized case of the 1980s. He was arrested and sent to prison to serve a four-year term. In his book *Journey into Darkness*, he recounts with horror the sounds of a cell block at night, the weeping of the homesick, the cursing of the angry, the screams of those being assaulted. He recalls the night that he found his way back to Christianity. "I had been lying on my bunk wide awake, thinking about the criminal bent my life had taken. I wondered whether I would ever be able to look honest people in the eye again. Some of the cocaine I'd smuggled into California had undoubtedly filtered its way down into young hands. I wondered how I could ever atone for that? Filled with emotion, I asked the Lord a question. 'Are you still there for someone like me?' I didn't exactly hear anything; it was more like being suddenly filled with a word. The word flowed through my body and soul . . . the word was 'Always.' "[4]

A therapist tells of counseling with a woman who shared that she had been sexually abused. The therapist recounts that the woman felt deep shame in telling her how, as an eight-year-old, climbing the dark stairwell in her apartment, she was molested by a neighbor. When he left her she began to weep and ever afterward had been deeply fearful. When the therapist prayed with her, she invited Jesus to go back to that little girl sitting on the stairs weeping and to fill her with his healing love. At this point the woman was thrilled to see Jesus loving and holding her as a wounded, weeping little child. With our Lord's help, she was gradually able to forgive her assailant and find freedom from the bondage of a shameful memory and the self-hatred it induced.[5]

Whom have you seen in your pre-Christmas travels around town? Inspired by the compassion of Qohelet, whose tears have you witnessed? The risen Christ is kneeling in prayer at the side of each person in pain. He embraces the woman covering a bruised eye with makeup. He is offering the gift of his presence to the widower. He is in the prisoner's cell. He is kneeling by the cot of the child in the homeless shelter. Will you join him there?

What tears are you silently shedding? He is also with you.

This baby, the gift for whom we are waiting this Advent, all grown up, crucified, resurrected, and present with us in the Person of the Holy Spirit is issuing to us this invitation for the days ahead: "Look, the tears of the oppressed. With my help, won't you comfort them?"

SERMON MODEL F—"THE ADVOCATE"

This sermon begins with a cultural proverb well known to a congregation that reinforces its self-esteem in the face of its suppression by a dominant culture. It sets this saying next to a biblical text that gives the community's self-esteem and striving a theological context, affirming God's advocacy for those society has tended to dismiss and challenging the community to persevere in faithful living in the face of obstacles. This text does not have to be proverbial, although it may well be.

Biblical subversive proverbs that could serve as textual partners with the congregation's proverb are, "The first shall be last and the last shall be first." "All who exalt themselves will be humbled, and all who humble themselves will be exalted" (Matt. 23:12; Luke 14:11). "Blessed are you who are poor, for yours is the kingdom of God" (Luke 6:20). "Many seek the favor of a ruler, but it is from the Lord that one gets justice" (Prov. 29:26). "Speak out for those who cannot speak, for the rights of all the destitute" (Prov. 31:8–9). (See also 11:4; 22:22–23; 23:10–11; 24:10–12.)

"It is God who drives away the flies from the cow who has no tail" might be paired with Psalm 86. "Well, I wouldn't take nothin' for my journey now," might be placed with Romans 5:1–5. "When whales battle, the shrimp's back is broken" could be paired with "The first shall be last and the last shall be first." The "better than" proverbs that affirm that poverty with integrity is superior to wealth and arrogance are a helpful resource (15:15–17; 16:8, 19; 18:10–12; 19:1), as well as those which affirm God's advocacy for the poor (14:20–21, 31; 15:25; 17:5; 19:17; 21:13; 22:9, 22–23; 29:7; 31:8, 9).

This model could be preached with good effect in congregations that are made up primarily of people from traditionally oppressed groups in racial or economic terms. It could also be preached in settings of relative affluence. These are the congregations in which I have done most of my ministry. As a white, middle-class heterosexual from a denomination that has been among the first to ordain women, my social location is not from within a traditionally oppressed group. However, I have been moved by the courage and perseverance of such groups within our culture, often expressed in proverbial terms. I discern in this wisdom a critique of aspects of dominant cultural and ecclesial worldviews. I discern in this proverbial wisdom an invitation to groups from a wide spectrum of social locations to become coworkers in the struggle for dignity and material survival of God's people. I believe that this "Advocate" sermon model is capable of issuing this combination challenge/invitation in a variety of congregational settings.

SERMON:
No One Who Looks Back Is Fit for the Kingdom:
"Keep Your Hand on the Plow"

> *Texts:* "No one who puts a hand to the plow and looks back is fit for the kingdom of God." (Luke 9:62)
>
> "Let us hold fast to the confession of our hope without wavering, for he who has promised is faithful." (Heb. 10:23)
>
> *Context:* Watch Night Service

Let's think back to the goals we set for ourselves last New Year's Eve. Some fell by the wayside in February or March. Others we saw through to their conclusion. Maybe we lost fifteen pounds, or prayed daily, or got our community involved in a local effort to fight crime. If we succeeded in reaching our goal, one quality that made all the difference was perseverance.

Perseverance was a quality my father sought to drum into all four of his children. He had been the youngest of a family of ten children that struggled through the Depression, and his father had drummed it into him, for he knew that whatever his young son was going to accomplish would have more to do with determination than inherited privilege. "A Fowler never gives up," he told my dad, who would later repeat it to us his children whenever he saw us on the brink of giving up on what he considered to be a worthy goal. He didn't overuse it, though. He knew that perseverance is only a good thing when it is properly motivated and directed toward a worthy goal.

Perseverance is a crucial quality for us Christians to cultivate in the year ahead, because we live in a society where not all perseverance is fueled by faith in God and directed toward the good of the community. Some is fueled by an arrogant desire to win at all costs. "I don't come here to play, I come here to win." "See you at the top!" "Second place means first place loser." Some perseverance is fueled by a desire to exploit others ("Do unto others before they do unto you"); some by a yen for revenge ("Don't get mad, get even"). A great deal of perseverance today is fueled by the pursuit of material possessions that make for a life rich in things and poor in soul ("The one who has the most toys when he dies, wins!").

Then there is the perseverance fueled by the desire for improving the quality of our lives in community in the best sense of the word quality: "Persistence prevails when all else fails" is one of my favorite proverbs. I like it because it rhymes and it's easy to remember when I feel like giving up. The Korean proverb "Fall down seven times and get up eight" expresses the quality of tenacity for which the Korean people are renowned.[6] I like that because it can help inspire us here tonight in the pursuit of an education, athletic achievement, a job, a decent level of material existence for one's family. These are goals many of us are working toward in our communities in the year that lies ahead, and rightly so.

Then there is the perseverance that is fueled by faith toward godly goals. Faith-fueled perseverance is a hallmark of the theology of African-American communities of faith. An often-heard saying is "The race is not to the swift nor the strong, but to him that endureth to the end." Perseverance continues to build communities' resolve and self-esteem.

"Cheer the weary traveler, along the heavenly way."[7] "Keep inchin' along, like a ol' inchworm" in preparation for when "Jesus is coming by and by." "I shall not, I shall not be moved, Just like a tree, planted by the waters" (Ps. 1:3). "Walk together, children, don't you get weary; There's a great camp meetin' in the Promised Land" (Gal. 6:9). The theme of not turning back sounds in "I'll never turn back no more, no more." "I have decided to follow Jesus; No turning back, no turning back." "Keep your hand on the plow [and] hold on!" (145).

This proverb captures the spirit of faith-fueled perseverance that has helped oppressed communities survive as they have struggled to embody Jesus Christ's presence in the here and now, persevering in the face of forces that would threaten their survival. "Keep your hand on the plow and hold on!" captures the challenge that African-American faith communities offer to other cultures and church traditions, a call to work together toward racial, economic, and gender justice.

"Keep your hand on the plow and hold on!" That's the only way any of us attained those godly goals we did attain from last New Year's Day. That's the only way communities struggle against economic injustice and racial and gender prejudice and survive. "Keep your hand on the plow and hold on!" That's the only way that segregation laws in this country were declared unconstitutional, that black women, traditionally discriminated against on the basis of race, gender, and economics, are claiming their voice and viewpoints in contemporary literature and ethics, that a group of mothers whose children have been killed by drunk drivers have worked for tougher laws, that activists got sexual harassment legislation put in place, that the epidemic of child poverty in this country is being battled, that discrimination against homosexuals will one day cease to be tolerated.

Perseverance in the context of our Christian life together is not just a desirable, success-enhancing personality trait, it is a crucial quality for disciples in proclaiming the kingdom of God. Jesus says that "No one who puts a hand to the plow and looks back is fit for the kingdom of God" (Luke 9:62). That would be just about all of us, wouldn't it? Haven't we all, at one time or another, felt our perseverance falter?

We're in good company at such times. On January 27, 1956, a young pastor sat in his kitchen in Montgomery, Alabama, holding a cup of coffee, unable to sleep. The bus boycott seemed to be collapsing. His own life had been repeatedly threatened. Earlier in the evening a caller had warned, "If you aren't out of this town in three days, we're going to blow your brains out and blow up your house." Then, as he later recounted:

"I bowed down over that cup of coffee. . . . I prayed a prayer and I prayed out loud that night. I said, 'Lord, I'm down here trying to do what's right. I think I'm right. I think the cause we represent is right. But Lord I must confess that I'm weak now. I'm faltering. I'm losing my courage. And I can't let the people see me like this because if they see me weak and losing my courage, they will begin to get weak.'" Martin Luther King Jr. needed the word of this proverb. "Keep your hand on the plow."[8]

A pastor tells of a small Presbyterian church that caught a fresh vision of the ministry it could offer to a rural region of intense need. Enthusiasm surged at first and then crashed. After just eighteen months the congregation's elders petitioned the denomination to close the church's doors. "We're exhausted. We just don't have the

resources to do what we thought we could."⁹ They needed the word
of this proverb: "Keep your hand on the plow."

"Jump at de sun—and you might at least catch hold to de moon,"
Lucy Potts Hurston, mother of Zora Neale Hurston, told her.¹⁰ After her mother's death Zora was passed from relative to relative and
had to make her own way in the world, in a lifelong battle against
what has been called the "triple oppression" of black women—economic, racial, and gender.¹¹ She became a novelist, folklorist, and an-
thropologist, one of the most prominent black women writers of the
Harlem literary renaissance between the world wars. Then, with her
work devalued by her male literary colleagues and patronized by
white publishers and unjustly accused of molesting a young boy, her
life and career went into free fall. She moved back to Florida where
she eked out a living as a maid, library clerk, substitute teacher, and
freelance writer. Poor, discouraged, and weary of rejection letters, she
wrote to her agent, "Just inching along like a stepped-on worm from
day to day. Borrowing a little here and there. . . . The humiliation is
getting too much for my self-respect, speaking from inside my soul.
I have tried to keep it to myself and just wait. To look and look at the
magnificent sweep of the Everglade, birds included, and keep a smile
on my face."¹²

Who is tempted to look back from their plowing? Those middle-
class Christians who are tempted to give up on ministry to the poor.
Ethicist Sharon Welch says that the temptation to cynicism and despair when problems are seen as intransigent is a temptation that takes
a particular form for the middle class. "The despair of the affluent, the
middle class, has a particular tone: it is a despair cushioned by privilege and grounded in privilege. It is easier to give up on long-term
social change when one is comfortable in the present—when it is possible to have challenging work, excellent health care and housing, and
access to the fine arts. When the good life is present or within reach,
it is tempting to despair of its ever being in reach for others and re-
sort to merely enjoying it for oneself and one's family. . . . Becoming
so easily discouraged is the privilege of those accustomed to too much
power, accustomed to having needs met without negotiation and
work, accustomed to having a political and economic system that re-
sponds to their needs."¹³

An old proverb says, "When you get to your wit's end, remember
that God lives there." And it's a good thing, too. Because it's not nat-

ural to pursue long and arduous journeys with unflagging bravery and energy. It's not humanly possible to keep on plowing, keep on proclaiming the kingdom of God without looking back. Except as we, moment by moment, follow the wise counsel of the author of Hebrews to a community tempted to turn back. "Let us hold fast to the confession of our hope without wavering, for he who has promised is faithful. And let us consider how to provoke one another to love and good deeds, not neglecting to meet together, as is the habit of some, but encouraging one another, and all the more as you see the Day approaching" (Heb. 10:23–25). Here is the faith that has fueled communities who live by the perseverance proverb "Keep your hand on the plow and hold on!"

The young pastor sitting at his kitchen table in the middle of a threatening night, praying to God for the gift of perseverance, felt another hand steadying his grasp on the plow.

"And it seemed at that moment that I could hear an inner voice saying to me, 'Martin Luther, stand up for righteousness. Stand up for justice. Stand up for truth. And lo I will be with you, even until the end of the world.' I heard the voice of Jesus saying still to fight on. He promised never to leave me alone" *(Upon This Rock,* 173). Keep your hand on the plow and hold on—how? By holding fast to the confession of our hope without wavering, for the one who has promised is faithful.

The little rural church that begged to close its doors was in for a shock. The denomination said, "Don't quit now. You may be on to something." After recovering from the shock of not being allowed to quit, the congregation said, "Well, maybe we are on to something!" Over the next years they held to their fundamental vision of being a community in ministry to the rural poor. They also learned unanticipated lessons about simplifying and focusing their efforts, letting go of their church building, developing lay leadership and worshiping in homes. For more than twenty years now that community has lived the way of healing love in a region of intense need. They have held fast to the confession of their hope without wavering, affirming that the one who has promised is faithful.[14]

The story of Zora Neale Hurston is not a "See you at the top!" success story of perseverance bringing a sudden turnaround of her fortunes. In 1959, Hurston suffered a severe stroke and entered a county welfare home, where she died three months later on January 28, 1960.

"Make a way out of no way" was the spirit instilled in novelist Alice Walker by her mother. Teaching Hurston's novel *Their Eyes Were Watching God* in a literature course at Wellesley College, Walker read in a folklore essay that Hurston was buried in an unmarked grave in the Garden of Heavenly Rest, a segregated cemetery in Fort Pierce, Florida. Outraged at this insult to Hurston, Walker headed south in August of 1973 determined to find Zora's grave. Making her way through waist-high weeds, she located the grave and laid on it a marker inscribed with the words: "Zora Neale Hurston/ 'A Genius of the South'/ Novelist/ Folklorist/ Anthropologist/ 1901–1960."[15] Thanks to the perseverance of Walker and others, Hurston today is "the most widely taught black woman writer in the canon of American literature." Hurston is one who met the triple oppression of black women with a threesome of resisting qualities shared by black women throughout their history of suppression: invisible dignity, quiet grace, and unshouted courage.[16]

In the heart of New York City, in a neighborhood of such poverty, crime, and despair that the police in the precinct wear T-shirts that say "The Killing Fields," St. Paul Community Baptist Church has a thriving ministry to people's spiritual and physical needs under the leadership of Pastor Johnny Youngblood. Pastor Youngblood calls it the Church Unusual. From the late seventies to the early nineties, the church has built affordable housing, created a school, replaced brothels and numbers joints with family stores. Through innovative programs it has made contact with those who have traditionally eluded the black church, from drug abusers to the neighborhood's youth and men.

It is December 23, 1990, the Sunday before Christmas. The yuletide spirit at St. Paul's was less one of celebration than one of struggle. In the deserts of Saudi Arabia more than a quarter-million American soldiers, including Sonia from this congregation, gathered for war against Iraqi forces that had occupied Kuwait. In offices and factories of America, thousands of people had been laid off, including Betty from this congregation, as the nation sank deeper into recession. In the streets and shops of New York, twelve people had been murdered in a single weekend, as the most violent year in the city's history neared its end.

St. Paul's is decorated with wreaths and poinsettias, and the choir is singing "Go Tell It on the Mountain." Pastor Johnny Ray Youngblood is meditatively looking out over his flock, preparing spiritually to administer Communion. There is a group called "The Fifty Black Churchmen" who have raised a pool of eighty thousand dollars for starting small businesses in the blocks around the church. There is Kathleen, grandmother to so many children that the saying "Blood is thicker than water" has no meaning. There is Annie, whose unarmed husband was recently killed by an off-duty policeman over a traffic squabble. There is Robert, who is leading a support group for former addicts, daily praying to stay clean himself. "The Overcoming Crowd, " Pastor Youngblood calls them in his prayers and to their faces.

The strains of the music fade, and Pastor Youngblood moves forward to consecrate the Communion elements. "Last night," he says to the people, "I was having a go-round with God. And I asked him, 'Why must I feel the compulsive urge to preach all these different angles on the gospel? Why do I have to make this church a Church Unusual? Why can't I just run with it the way I heard it as a child?' And the Lord didn't answer.

"But I know the Lord answers in his own time. . . . So we celebrate the Lord's sacrifice. We receive the emblems of his broken body and his shed blood." Pastor Youngblood brings the cracker to his mouth and says, "Let's eat together." He touches the grape juice to his lips and says, "Let's drink together." He turns to face the organist, Eli Wilson.

And against bigotry and poverty and murder and war, against the gates of hell, he says, "Mr. Wilson, let's go down singing."

And if this Overcoming Crowd could pick one line to sing it could well be this one: "Keep your hand on the plow and hang on!" (361–63).

John Wesley's Covenant Renewal Service, with which we begin this New Year together, gives us a key admonition as we make a fresh start.

"Resolve to be faithful. You have given to the Lord your hearts, you have opened your mouths to the Lord, and you have dedicated yourself to God. With God's power, never go back."[17]

Let us hold fast the confession of our hope without wavering, for the one who has promised is faithful! Working together toward Godly goals in the year ahead, let us keep our hand on the plow and hold on!

Notes

Introduction: The Preacher as Sage

1. Thomas G. Long, *Preaching and the Literary Forms of the Bible* (Philadelphia: Fortress Press, 1989), 55.
2. This definition is attributed to Cervantes and is quoted by James Crenshaw in *Old Testament Wisdom: An Introduction* (Atlanta: John Knox Press, 1981), 67.
3. Long, 54.
4. Ibid, 57.
5. This definition is quoted by Crenshaw in *Old Testament Wisdom,* 67.
6. William McKane, *Proverbs: A New Approach* (Philadelphia: Westminster Press, 1970), 23.
7. Garrison Keillor, "Roy Bradley, Boy Broadcaster," in *The Book of Guys: Stories by Garrison Keillor* (New York: Viking Press, 1993), 149.
8. Long, 57–58.
9. Tex Sample, *Ministry in an Oral Culture: Living with Will Rogers, Uncle Remus, and Minnie Pearl* (Louisville, Ky.: Westminster John Knox Press, 1994), 11–12.
10. Leonora Tubbs Tisdale, *Preaching as Local Theology and Folk Art* (Minneapolis: Fortress Press, 1996).
11. Robin Tolmach Lakoff, "Some of My Favorite Writers Are Literate: The Mingling of Oral and Literate Strategies in Written Communication," in *Spoken and Written Language: Exploring Orality and Literacy,* ed. Deborah Tannen (Norwood, N.J.: Albex Publishing Corp., 1982), 255, 57.
12. Alan Dundes, "Folk Ideas as Units of Worldview," in *Essays in Folkloristics* (Kailash Puri Meerut: Ved Prakash Vatuk. Folklore Institute, 1978), 105–20.
13. Roland E. Murphy, *The Tree of Life: An Exploration of Biblical Wisdom Literature,* The Anchor Bible Reference Library, ed. David Noel Freedman (New York: Doubleday, 1990), 4.
14. "Wisdom in person" is the designation given to Jesus by Ben Witherington, III, in his book *Jesus the Sage: The Pilgrimage of Wisdom* (Minneapolis: Fortress Press, 1994), 147ff.

Chapter 1: What Makes Proverbs Work

1. "Wisdom," in *Old Testament Form Criticism,* ed. John H. Hayes, Trinity University Monograph Series in Religion, 2, ed. John H. Hayes (San Antonio: Trinity University Press, 1974), 230.

2. Bernard Brandon Scott, *Hear Then the Parable: A Commentary on the Parables of Jesus* (Minneapolis: Fortress Press, 1989), 42.

3. Roland E. Murphy, *Wisdom Literature: Job, Proverbs, Ruth, Canticles, Ecclesiastes, and Esther* (Grand Rapids: Wm. B. Eerdmans Publishing Co., 1981), The Forms of the Old Testament Literature, 13, ed. Rolf Knierim and Gene M. Tucker, 4–6.

4. See James Williams's "Excursus: Aphorism and Proverb," in *Those Who Ponder Proverbs: Aphoristic Thinking and Biblical Literature* (Sheffield: Almond Press, 1981), 78f.

5. The instances of proverb use in the historical writings, the Wisdom of Solomon, and Sirach show the proverbs performing primarily, as they do in the book of Proverbs, in the role of confirming normative, prevailing values. Proverbs occur in the book of Job, at times to challenge normative wisdom, but they are not the chief mode of expression in their own right. Williams, *Those Who Ponder Proverbs,* 15–16.

6. *Proverbs East and West: An Anthology of Chinese, Korean, and Japanese Sayings with Western Equivalents,* comp. Kim Yong-Chol (Elizabeth, N.J.: Hollym International Corporation, 1991), 85.

7. Beatrice Silverman-Weinreich, "Towards a Structural Analysis of Yiddish Proverbs," in *The Wisdom of Many: Essays on the Proverb,* ed. Wolfgang Mieder and Alan Dundes (New York: Garland Publishing, 1981), 65–85.

8. Alan Dundes, "On the Structure of the Proverb," in *The Wisdom of Many: Essays on the Proverb,* 60.

9. *Proverbs East and West,* 158.

10. The discussion that follows draws on Alan Dundes, "On the Structure of the Proverb," 53ff.

11. Paul Ricoeur, "The Metaphorical Process," *Semeia* 4 (1975): 76.

12. Neal R. Norrick, *How Proverbs Mean: Semantic Studies in English Proverbs,* Trends in Linguistics: Studies and Monographs, 27, ed. Werner Winter (Berlin: Walter de Gruyter, 1985), 49.

13. Sallie McFague, *Metaphorical Theology: Models of God in Religious Language* (Philadelphia: Fortress Press, 1982), 36.

14. Ricoeur, "The Metaphorical Process," 79.

15. This definition is attributed to English statesman Lord John Russell and is quoted by Dundes, "On the Structure of the Proverb," 61.

Chapter 2: What Proverbs Do

1. James L. Crenshaw, "Wisdom and Authority: Sapiential Rhetoric and Its Warrants," Supplements to Vetus Testamentum, 32 (1981), 10–29.
2. William R. Bascom, "Four Functions of Folklore," *Journal of American Folklore* 67 (1954): 333–49.
3. Joseph Raymond, "Tensions in Proverbs: More Light on International Understanding," *The Wisdom of Many: Essays on the Proverb,* ed. Wolfgang Mieder and Alan Dundes (New York: Garland Publishing, 1981), 301.
4. Leo Perdue, "The Social Character of Paraenesis and Paraenetic Literature," *Semeia* 50 (1990): 5–39.
5. A concern for order, or respectability, is the hallmark of the worldview of a segment of the working class that Tex Sample calls "Blue-Collar Respectables." The marks of respectability are "the intactness and well-being of the family; enough money to provide some of the luxuries of life as well as security; and a hankering after respectability and acceptance." Tex Sample, *Blue-Collar Ministry: Facing Economic and Social Realities of Working People* (Valley Forge, Pa.: Judson Press, 1984), 80. Respectability involves a conventional morality that commends moderation and trustworthiness and condemns associating with people who have bad reputations. It is based, to a large degree, on the proverbial conviction that "you reap what you sow." (76). Respectability is motivated by a desire for dignity and self-respect.
6. James Williams, *Those Who Ponder Proverbs: Aphoristic Thinking and Biblical Literature* (Sheffield: Almond Press, 1981),17. The proverbs of Confucianism, influential in the cultural substructures of China's neighbors Japan, Korea, and Vietnam, display the marks of a wisdom of order. Their emphasis is on obedience to elders and rulers toward the goal of social order. These Confucian thought modes, espoused by first-generation Korean-American immigrants, are being challenged by the second and third generations in contemporary Korean-American congregations.
7. Edward H. Schroeder, "Korean Women Search for the Silver Coin," *Christian Century,* May 2, 1990, 452–54.
8. Wolfgang Mieder, "Proverbs in Nazi Germany: The Promulgation of Anti-Semitism and Stereotypes through Folklore," *Proverbs Are Never out of Season: Popular Wisdom in the Modern Age* (New York: Oxford University Press, 1993), 242.
9. Perdue, "The Social Character of Paraenesis," 8–9.
10. Wolfgang Mieder, "Proverbs Everyone Ought to Know: Paremiological Minimum and Cultural Literacy," in *Proverbs Are Never out of Season,* 47.
11. Wolfgang Mieder, "Proverb Parodies," *American Proverbs: A Study of Texts and Contexts* (New York: Peter Lang, 1989), 239f.

12. John J. Collins, "Proverbial Wisdom and the Yahwist Vision," *Semeia* 17 (1980): 6.
13. Elizabeth Faith Huwiler, "Control of Reality in Israelite Wisdom: A Contextual Study," Ph.D. diss., Duke University Divinity School, 1988.
14. Peter Seitel, "Proverbs: A Social Use of Metaphor," *Genre* 2 (1969): 143–61.
15. Collins, 6.

Chapter 3: How to Create Sermons on Proverbs

1. Wolfgang Iser, *The Act of Reading: A Theory of Aesthetic Response* (Baltimore: Johns Hopkins University Press, 1978), 94–97.
2. Works that explore the import of proverbial clusters for interpretation of individual verses include R. N. Whybray, *The Composition of the Book of Proverbs* (Sheffield: JSOT Press, 1994); Elizabeth Huwiler, "Control of Reality in Israelite Wisdom: A Contextual Study" (Ph.D. diss., Duke University Divinity School, 1988); Raymond C. van Leeuwen, *Context and Meaning in Proverbs 25—27*, SBLDS 96 (Atlanta: Scholars Press, 1988); John Dominic Crossan, *In Fragments: The Aphorisms of Jesus* (San Francisco: Harper & Row, 1983); and Robert C. Tannehill, *The Sword of His Mouth: Forceful and Imaginative Language in Synoptic Sayings* (Philadelphia: Fortress Press, 1975).

Chapter 4: Biblical Proverbs That Create Order

1. Roland E. Murphy, *Wisdom Literature: Job, Proverbs, Ruth, Canticles, Ecclesiastes, and Esther* (Grand Rapids: William B. Eerdmans Publishing Co., 1981), The Forms of the Old Testament Literature, 13, ed. Rolf Knierim and Gene M. Tucker, 48–49.
2. Roland E. Murphy, *The Tree of Life: An Exploration of Biblical Wisdom Literature,* The Anchor Bible Reference Library (New York: Doubleday, 1990), 22–23.
3. Thomas P. McCreesh, O.P., "Wisdom as Wife: Proverbs 31:10–31," *Revue Biblique* (1985): 25–46.
4. Linguistic and structural evidence suggest a postexilic editing. Patrick Skehan, "A Single Editor for the Whole Book of Proverbs," in *Studies in Ancient Israelite Wisdom,* The Library of Biblical Studies, ed. Harry M. Orlinsky (New York: Ktav Publishing House, 1976), 329–40.
5. Harold C. Washington, "Wealth and Poverty in the Instruction of Amenemope and the Hebrew Proverbs: Two Test Cases in the Social Location and Function of Ancient Near Eastern Wisdom Literature," Ph.D. diss., Princeton Theological Seminary, 1992, 239ff.
6. Claudia V. Camp, *Wisdom and the Feminine in the Book of Proverbs,* Bible and Literature Series, 11 (Sheffield: Almond Press, 1985), 107.
7. Prov. 3:22; 8:35; 10:27; 13:14; 21:21; 22:4.

8. Prov. 13:3; 16:17; 19:16; 29:10.

9. See John B. White's article "The Sages' Strategy to Preserve *Shalom*," in *The Listening Heart: Essays in Wisdom and the Psalms in Honor of Roland E. Murphy, O. Carm.*, Journal for the Study of the Old Testament Supplements, 58 (Sheffield: Sheffield Academic Press, 1987), 299–311.

10. Walther Zimmerli, "The Place and Limit of Wisdom in the Framework of Old Testament Theology," in *Studies in Ancient Israelite Wisdom*, 314–26.

11. Norman Habel, "The Symbolism of Wisdom in Proverbs 1—9," *Interpretation* 26 (1972): 131–57.

12. Roland Murphy, "Wisdom Theses," in *Wisdom and Knowledge*, ed. J. Armenti. (Villanova, Pa.: Villanova University Press, 1976), 198.

13. Prov. 10:6–11; 11:9; 12:6; 12:18; 13:2.

14. Elizabeth Faith Huwiler, "Control of Reality in Israelite Wisdom: A Contextual Study," Ph.D. diss., Duke University Divinity School, 1988, 182–239.

15. Prov. 14:20; 19:4, 7; 22:7; 28:3. J. David Pleins, "Poverty in the Social World of the Wise," *Journal for the Study of the Old Testament* 37 (1987): 67.

16. Prov. 6:6–11; 10:4; 12:11; 14:23; 19:15, 24; 20:4, 13; 21:5, 17; 23:20; 24:34. The attempt to locate poverty in laziness is entirely absent from the prophetic literature. Pleins, 68.

17. F. Charles Fensham, "Widow, Orphan and the Poor in Ancient Near Eastern Legal and Wisdom Literature," in *Studies in Ancient Israelite Wisdom*, 170.

18. Washington, "Wealth and Poverty," 303. See Prov. 14:31; 15:25; 19:17; 22:9, 16, 22–23.

19. Robert Gordis, "The Social Background of Wisdom Literature," in *Poets, Prophets, and Sages: Essays in Biblical Interpretation* (Bloomington: Indiana University Press, 1971), 178.

20. Huwiler, 242f.

21. Murphy, "Wisdom Theses," 198–99.

22. Claudia Camp argues that women's contributions in the postexilic period were supported and authorized because it was in the larger social interest to do so. "If Proverbs 1—9 envisions a degree of female authority and equality, it is still authority and equality granted by men— and reclaimed by them not long thereafter." Claudia V. Camp, "Paraenesis: A Feminist Response," *Semeia* 50 (1990): 243f. See also Carol A. Newsom, "Woman and the Discourse of Patriarchal Wisdom: A Study of Proverbs 1—9," in *Gender and Difference in Ancient Israel*, ed. Peggy L. Day (1989).

23. John Collins, "Proverbial Wisdom and the Yahwist Vision," *Semeia* 40 (1980): 10.

24. Roland Murphy, "Wisdom and Creation," *Journal of Biblical Literature* 104 (1985): 3–11. The Wisdom tradition represented by Proverbs, even

when it uses the term YHWH as a designation for God, does not have in mind a patron deity who had entered into an intimate relationship with the nation Israel or any of its official representatives. Instead, YHWH functioned as an equivalent of El or *Elohim,* the more general names for God. James L. Crenshaw, "The Concept of God in Old Testament Wisdom," in *In Search of Wisdom: Essays in Memory of John G. Gammie* (Louisville, Ky.: Westminster John Knox Press, 1993), 7–8.

25. Gerhard von Rad, *Wisdom in Israel,* trans. James D. Martin (Nashville: Abingdon Press, 1972), 62.

26. Frederick M. Wilson, "Sacred and Profane? The Yahwistic Redaction of Proverbs Reconsidered," in *The Listening Heart,* 328.

27. Ibid., 322f. "Do you see persons wise in their own eyes? There is more hope for fools than for them" (Prov. 26:12).

28. Collins, 11.

29. Murphy, *The Tree of Life,* 114–15.

30. These three affirmations compose the theological framework of Proverbs. Frederick Wilson, "Sacred and Profane?" 329–31.

31. According to Gerhard von Rad, the injunction to fear the Lord "contains in a nutshell the whole Israelite theory of knowledge. . . . She was . . . of the opinion that effective knowledge about God is the only thing that puts a man [*sic*] into a right relationship with the objects of his perception." *Wisdom in Israel,* 67–68.

32. Roland E. Murphy, "The Faith of Qohelet," *Word and World* 7 (1987): 256.

33. Wilson, 330.

34. Camp, *Wisdom and the Feminine,* 227–31.

35. James Williams, *Those Who Ponder Proverbs: Aphoristic Thinking and Biblical Literature* (Sheffield: Almond Press, 1981), 18–32.

36. Alan Jenks, "Theological Presuppositions," *Horizons in Biblical Theology,* 7, no. 1 (June 1985): 43–44.

37. Camp, *Wisdom and the Feminine,* 215ff.

38. All biblical quotations are from the NRSV Bible.

39. Prov. 12:9; 15:16–17; 16:8, 16, 19; 17:1, 12; 19:1; 21:3, 9, 19: 25:24; 27:10c; 28:6; 22:1, listed in *Old Testament Form Criticism,* ed. John H. Hayes, Trinity University Monograph Series in Religion, 2, ed. John H. Hayes (San Antonio, Tex.: Trinity University Press, 1974), 238.

40. "All our steps are ordered by the Lord; how then can we understand our own ways?" (Prov. 20:24). See Job 28:12; 38:19; Eccl. 7:13, 24.

Chapter 5: Biblical Proverbs That Subvert Order

1. This is the approach taken by Michael V. Fox in his *Qohelet and His Contradictions* (Sheffield: Almond Press, 1989). He describes alternative interpretations on pp. 19–28.

2. R. N. Whybray, "The Identification and Use of Quotations in Ecclesiastes," Supplements to Vetus Testamentum, 32: (1981), 435–51.
3. Roland E. Murphy, "Qohelet's 'Quarrel' with the Fathers," in *From Faith to Faith* (Pittsburgh, Pa.: Pickwick Press, 1979), 236. R. N. Whybray, in "The Identification and Use of Quotations in Ecclesiastes," concurs: "Qoheleth's purpose in quoting these sayings was not to demonstrate their falsity. He quoted them because he accepted their truth" (p. 450).
4. Quotations from Ecclesiastes in this chapter are from the NRSV.
5. C. L. Seow, *Ecclesiastes*, Anchor Bible (New York: Doubleday, 1996), 3:246. The name Ecclesiastes is the Latin transliteration of the Greek *ekklēsiastēs*, a word referring to a member of the citizen's assembly *(ekklēsia)* (1:1).
6. On the relationship of prophecy and apocalyptic in the postexilic period, see David E. Aune, *Prophecy in Early Christianity and the Ancient Mediterranean World* (Grand Rapids: Wm. B. Eerdmans Publishing Co., 1983), 112ff. While the discontinuity between the two genres must be noted, most of the essential features of apocalyptic literature that flourished from 200 B.C. to A.D. 100 have roots in the prophetic literature of the 6th and 5th centuries B.C.
7. The relationship between apocalyptic and wisdom in the postexilic period is addressed in *The Sage in Israel and the Ancient Near East,* ed. John G. Gammie and Leo G. Perdue. (Winona Lake, Ind.: Eisenbrauns, 1990), Sect. 5, "The Sage from Before the Close of the Hebrew Canon to Post-Biblical Times." See especially John J. Collins, "The Sage in the Apocalyptic and Pseudepigraphic Literature," 343–45.
8. Seow, 3:283–84.
9. Leo G. Perdue, "The Social Character of Paraenesis and Paraenetic Literature," *Semeia* 50 (1990): 9.
10. Ibid.
11. Robert Gordis attributes Qoheleth's lack of active response to injustice to the fact that "he personally found life tolerable even under the conditions he deprecated." "The Wisdom of Koheleth," *Poets, Prophets, and Sages: Essays in Biblical Interpretation* (Bloomington: Indiana University Press, 1971), 340.
12. Murphy, "The Faith of Qoheleth," 255. *Elohim* occurs 40 times in Ecclesiastes, and it is the preferred designation for the deity in the wisdom tradition over YHWH, the specific name of Israel's God. Seow, *Ecclesiastes,* 2:161.
13. Seow, 2:136.
14. The term "work of God" is frequently used of the high points of divine activity, especially in the Psalms (66:3; 92:5; 111:2, 7; 118:17). There is a clear note of awe about the works of God, especially human beings, in Ps. 139:14, and the wisdom of God in all God's created works is hailed

in Ps. 104:24 ("How manifold are your works, O Lord! In wisdom you have wrought them all") Murphy, "Qohelet's 'Quarrel' with the Fathers," 238.

15. James Williams interprets *hāʿōlām* as whatever lies at the core of existence, eternity, the earth, love of the world, true wisdom, everlasting life. It is that which moves human beings toward God. Williams believes that *ʿōlām* for Qohelet is the hidden mystery of the whole, the "foundation" of the earth's remaining, the deepest source of human striving. It is the opposite of *hebel*. "What Does It Profit a Man?" 378.

16. Murphy, "Qohelet's 'Quarrel,'" 239.

17. "For what will it profit them if they gain the whole world but forfeit their life?" (Matt. 16:26; Mark 8:36). In this New Testament context the vaporous quality of existence is recognized within the call to discipleship and hope in the Son of Man and the kingdom of God. Williams, "What Does It Profit a Man?" 383.

18. James G. Williams points out that "Koheleth does not consider how the severely oppressed" (whom he takes into account in 4:1ff.) "might enjoy their toil, eating and drinking, and human relationships, when they are obviously in a state of extreme deprivation. This may reflect an upper class background and conservative orientation." "What Does It Profit a Man?" 190, n. 39.

19. Seow, *Ecclesiastes,* vol. 3, 346–47.

20. Fox, *Qohelet and His Contradictions,*15. See also R. N. Whybray's "Qoheleth, Preacher of Joy," *Journal for the Study of the Old Testament* 23 (1982): 87–98. Whybray argues that Qohelet, far from being a teacher of unrelieved pessimism, recommended joy in the precarious and precious present moment. He regards this as Qohelet's last word.

21. Murphy, "The Faith of Qoheleth," 256.

22. James G. Williams believes that Qohelet derives his fear of God through the twofold experience of the inscrutability of God's workings and the dissolution of a world order that rewards righteousness. "What Does It Profit a Man?" 380.

23. Roland E. Murphy, "The Faith of Qoheleth," 256.

24. Murphy, "Qohelet's Quarrel with the Fathers," 241. In Proverbs, the fear of the Lord is a fountain of life, so that one may avoid the snares of death (14:27; 13:14; 4:6, 7). In Qoheleth the fear of the Lord is a response to the realization that death comes to wise person and fool alike.

25. Michael V. Fox, *Qohelet and His Contradictions,* 29. Pss. 62:9; 78:33; Isa. 57:13.

26. Seow, *Ecclesiastes,* 3:275.

27. Fox, *Qohelet and His Contradictions,* 32.

28. Fox, *Qohelet and His Contradictions,* 34.

29. "For there is no enduring remembrance of the wise or of fools, seeing that in the days to come all will have been long forgotten," 2:16.

30. Seow, *Ecclesiastes,* 3:346–47.

31. Williams, "What Does It Profit a Man?" 375–89.

32. Seow, *Ecclesiastes,* 2:123.

33. Other synonymous parallel proverbs that confirm normative wisdom are: "Even when fools walk on the road, they lack sense, and show to everyone that they are fools" (10:3). "Fools fold their hands and consume their own flesh" (4:5).

34. "Wisdom excels folly as light excels darkness" (2:13). "Better is a poor but wise youth than an old but foolish king, who will no longer take advice" (4:13). "To draw near to listen is better than the sacrifice offered by fools" (5:5). "It is better that you should not vow than that you should vow and not fulfill it" (5:5). "Better is the sight of the eyes than the wandering of desire" (6:9). "It is better to hear the rebuke of the wise than to hear the song of fools" (7:5).

35. Seow, *Ecclesiastes,* 4:443.

36. Graham S. Ogden, "Qoheleth's Use of the 'Nothing Is Better' Form," *Journal of Biblical Literature* 98 (1979): 339–41.

37. Gerhard von Rad, *Wisdom in Israel,* trans. James D. Martin (Nashville: Abingdon Press, 1972), 231.

38. See Job 21:22; 28:12.

39. According to James Crenshaw, "Impossible questions fanned the flames of pessimism and heightened the theodicy question for ancient Israelites accustomed to solving most questions." Compare Qohelet 7:24 with Deut. 30:11–14, and Job 28:28 with Job 28:12. "Impossible Questions, Sayings, and Tasks," *Semeia* (1980): 29–30.

40. See also Eccl. 2:25; 3:22; 5:11; 6:8,12–13; 8:1; 10:14.

41. Murphy, "Qohelet's 'Quarrel,'" 235.

42. Gordis, "Quotations in Biblical, Oriental, and Rabbinic Literature," *Poets, Prophets, and Sages,* 135–37.

43. See Gordis, "Quotations in Biblical, Oriental, Rabbinic Literature," 135–39, for an account of Qohelet's use of proverbial sayings as texts with ironic comment and his use of contrasting proverbs.

44. Qohelet repeatedly refers to toil and its products as *hebel* because the fruits of the toil of a wise person often go to a fool (2:18–26). See also 4:7–8; 6:1–2.

45. Whybray, "The Identification and Use," 450.

Chapter 6: Jesus' Subversive Sayings

1. In some cases, similar material is found in Mark. Q and Mark probably received the same oral or written traditions independently of each other. Ivan Havener, *Q: The Sayings of Jesus* (Collegeville, Minn.: Liturgical

Press, 1990), 26. A synopsis of Mark and Q traditions appears on pp. 160–61 of Havener.

2. Charles Carlston, "Proverbs, Maxims and the Historical Jesus," *Journal of Biblical Literature* 99 (March 1980): 80.

3. Q bears similarities to Hellenistic handbooks of instruction, combinations of maxims, proverbs, injunctions, and chreia. Chreia were a type of anecdote used in popular philosophy of the Greco-Roman world consisting of the description of a situation, followed by a philosopher's pointed aphoristic remark which offered social critique. Some scholars have concluded that Jesus was an itinerant Cynic philosopher-sage. While the parallels are instructive, the equation has several problems: it doesn't adequately depict Jesus' motivations for his subversive ministry; it fails to account for his death in other than accidental terms, and it doesn't adequately acknowledge the Hebrew roots of subversive wisdom. While Jesus' teachings, like the Cynics', eschew appeal to traditional authorities of the "fathers," unlike theirs, Jesus' teachings do not place at their center the overarching theme of Cynicism: self-sufficiency. Q's primary home, in my view, is in the milieu of Hebrew wisdom traditions. Stephen J. Patterson, "Wisdom in Q and Thomas," *In Search of Wisdom: Essays in Memory of John G. Gammie*, ed. Leo G. Perdue, Bernard Brandon Scott, William Johnston Wiseman (Louisville, Ky.: Westminster/John Knox Press, 1993), 206.

4. James M. Robinson, "Logoi Sophon: On the Gattung of Q," *Trajectories through Early Christianity* (Philadelphia: Fortress Press, 1971), 71–113. Robinson's classification of Q is disputed by scholars who assume that the subversive nature of its sayings makes the tradition more prophetic than sapiential in character. Patterson, "Wisdom in Q and Thomas," 205–6. The *Gospel of Thomas* is a Gnostic collection of sayings with marked similarities to Q, but in it there is no mention of the apocalyptic Son of Man and the focus is on the revelation of secret divine wisdom through Jesus' sayings.

5. Luke 7:33–35/Matt. 11:18–19.

6. James M. Robinson, "Jesus as Sophos and Sophia: Wisdom Tradition and the Gospels," *Aspects of Wisdom in Judaism and Early Christianity,* ed. R. L. Wilken (South Bend, Ind.: University of Notre Dame Press, 1975), 3, 4. See Luke 11:49–51; 13:34a/Matt. 23:34–37a.

7. Robinson, "Logoi Sophon: On the Gattung of Q," 71–113.

8. Arland D. Jacobson, *The First Gospel: An Introduction to Q* (Sonoma, Calif.: Polebridge Press, 1992), 2–4.

9. Robinson, "Jesus as Sophos," 13.

10. Arland Jacobson, *The First Gospel;* John S. Kloppenborg, *The Formation of Q: Trajectories in Ancient Wisdom Collections* (Philadelphia: Fortress Press, 1987).

11. Luke 6:20b–49; 9:57–62; 10:2–16, 21–24; 11:2–4, 9–13; 12:2–12, 22–34; 13:24–30, 34–35; 14:16–24, 26–27, 34–35; 17:33.
12. Luke 3:7–9, 16b–17; 7:1–10, 18–23, 24–26, 31–35; 11:14–15, 17–18a, 24–26, 27–28, 39b-44, 46–52; 12:42b–46; 17:34.
13. Jacobson, *The First Gospel*, 257.
14. This is the position taken by Burton Mack in his *The Lost Gospel: The Book of Q and Christian Origins* (New York: HarperCollins Publishers), 1993.
15. Examples include *1 Enoch, 2 Enoch,* and the *Testaments of the Twelve Patriarchs.* John J. Collins, "Wisdom, Apocalypticism, and Generic Compatibility," in *In Search of Wisdom: Essays in Memory of John G. Gammie,* 174–79.
16. The subject headings of the clusters are taken from Burton Mack's reconstruction in *The Lost Gospel: The Book of Q and Christian Origins,* which substantially agrees with John S. Kloppenborg's reconstruction in *Q Parallels: Synopsis, Critical Notes and Concordance.* (Sonoma, Calif.: Polebridge Press, 1988). The numberings of the entries from Q have been adapted to agree with Kloppenborg's segmentation of Q. Scholars agree that, to a greater degree than Matthew, Luke retains the original sequence of Q. They are divided, however, over which gospel generally retains the wording of individual verses more closely. The limits of this discussion do not permit debate about each saying. Such a debate is presented in Q Parallels. I have noted the Matthean differences from the Lukan at some key points.
17. Matthew has "Blessed are the poor in spirit." The woes, which immediately follow the blessings in Luke, are probably from Q, but were omitted by Matthew, perhaps because he felt them inappropriate for catechetical purposes in his Sermon on the Mount, including them in chapter 23 in the context of a diatribe against the Pharisees. Kloppenborg, *Q Parallels,* 26.
18. "Be merciful, just as your Father is merciful" (Luke 6:36). Matthew has "Be perfect, therefore, as your heavenly Father is perfect" (5:48).
19. Matthew places these sayings in the context of warning against false prophets, and the consequences of not bearing good fruit (7:19) are being "cut down and thrown into the fire."
20. Luke has the parable of the friend at midnight (11:5–8) immediately before these aphorisms on asking. Most scholars assert that this parable is from Q but was omitted by Matthew, perhaps because he thought it added nothing to the teaching that follows. Kloppenborg, *Q Parallels,* 88. Matthew 7:11 has "give good things" in lieu of Luke's "give the Holy Spirit" (Luke 11:13).
21. Matthew adds "the kingdom of God and his righteousness" (6:33).
22. In what is probably his edited version of a Q parable, Matthew emphasizes that the householder was a king, that the occasion was a wedding

banquet for his son, and that those who rejected the invitation also killed the king's messengers, and, finally, that, in retribution, the king sent soldiers to destroy the murderers and burn their city.

23. James Crenshaw, "Wisdom and Authority: Sapiential Rhetoric and Its Warrants," Supplements to Vetus Testamentum, 32 (1981), 10–29.
24. See Burton Mack's listing of aphorisms on pp. 110–11 of *The Lost Gospel*. Those sayings marked with an asterisk indicate my additions to Mack's listing. The sayings below are from the Lukan version of the sayings, from the NRSV.
25. Stephen J. Patterson, "The End of Apocalypse: Rethinking the Eschatological Jesus," *Theology Today*, April 1995, 46. Elisabeth Schüssler Fiorenza prefers to retain the Greek term *basileia* rather than to translate it kingdom. By this she keeps alive the political-social implications of the Jesus movement's challenge to the Roman empire, rather than referring only to the imperial activity of God. *Jesus: Miriam s Child, Sophia s Prophet* (New York: Continuum, 1995), 92.
26. Fiorenza, *Jesus: Miriam s Child*, 93. The egalitarianism of the Q community needs to be qualified in light of the relegation of women in Q1 to the role of support of the mendicant males. While the message of Q would have appealed to women, it is by no means evident that the instruction of Q1, couched in largely masculine rhetoric, is actually addressed to them. Women appear to have been given a greater role as the community faced opposition, about the time they made the identification of Jesus with heavenly Wisdom. Amy J. Levine, "Who's Catering the Q Affair?" *Semeia* 50 (1990): 150.
27. Patterson, *The End of Apocalypse*, 46.
28. Kloppenborg, *The Formation of Q*, 318.
29. Mack, *The Lost Gospel*, 111–12.
30. Levine, "Who's Catering the Q Affair?" 148.
31. James G. Williams, *Those Who Ponder Proverbs: Aphoristic Thinking and Biblical Literature* (Sheffield: Almond Press, 1981), 51.
32. William Beardslee, "The Wisdom Tradition and the Synoptic Gospels," *Journal of the American Academy of Religion* 35 (1967): 236.
33. Leo Perdue, "The Wisdom Sayings of Jesus," *Forum* 2 (1986): 6–7.
34. Carlston, "Proverbs, Maxims," 87–105.
35. Havener, *Q: The Sayings of Jesus*, 50.
36. Sirach 24, Wisdom of Solomon 7—9. God sends Sophia to "pitch her tent" and dwell in Israel as the revelation of the Torah (Sir. 24:8). She performs the same actions in the history of Israel that had been attributed to Yahweh in earlier scriptures (Wisd. 10–11:1).
37. Leo D. Lefebure, "Sophia: Wisdom and Christian Theology," *Christian Century*, Oct. 19, 1994, 953. See Ben Witherington III's study *Jesus the*

Sage: The Pilgrimage of Wisdom (Minneapolis: Fortress Press, 1994), chaps. 1 and 2.

38. The hymn in Colossians 1 develops this more extensively, applying the characteristics of Sophia to the cosmic Christ (1:15–20). The Epistle to the Hebrews also presents Christ in the role of Sophia (1:2–3). Lefebure, "Sophia," 954.

39. Fourth-century theologian Marius Victorinus understood Sophia as a name for all three persons of the Trinity, accepting both Logos and Sophia as names for the Son. Sophia is truly divine and thus can be addressed in prayer as a name for the triune God. Augustine interpreted Sophia in the Septuagint as the second person of the Trinity and described her as being sent by the Father to become incarnate (*On the Trinity* 4.5.27). Lefebure, "Sophia," 955.

40. Lefebure, "Sophia," 955–56. Sophia imagery figures prominently in the feminist Christologies of Isabel Carter Heyward and Rita Nakashima Brock. Both use "Christa," the name given to a statue of the female Jesus, arms outstretched as though crucified, sculpted by Edwina Sandys, in naming Jesus for contemporary women. Brock seeks to move Christology from its focus on a lone, heroic male savior figure to its locus in "Christa/Community," the gathering of those empowered by the Spirit-Sophia who live "by heart." These contemporary feminist christological appropriations of Sophia are discussed and critically evaluated by Elisabeth Schüssler Fiorenza in *Jesus: Miriam s Child, Sophia s Prophet,* 50–57.

41. William Beardslee, "The Uses of the Proverb in the Synoptic Gospels," *Interpretation* 24 (1970).

42. Carlston, "Proverbs, Maxims, and the Historical Jesus," 102.

43. The subversive proverbs advocating faith over an anxious brand of foresight build on references to the birds of the air and the lilies of the field (Matt. 6:25ff).

44. Similitudes come in the parables of the kingdom, in which, interestingly, the kingdom is subversively compared to the humble mustard shrub (Mark) and to leaven, a metaphor for moral corruption in the ancient world. Bernard Brandon Scott, "Jesus as Sage: An Innovating Voice in Common Wisdom," in *The Sage in Israel and the Ancient Near East,* ed. John G. Gammie and Leo G. Perdue (Winona Lake, Ind.: Eisenbrauns, 1990), 409ff. Here aspects of the natural world as they are commonly understood are brought in to undercut or defamiliarize hearers to normative wisdom's order and expectation.

45. Perdue, "The Wisdom Sayings of Jesus," 10–11.

46. Robert C. Tannehill, *The Sword of His Mouth: Forceful and Imaginative Language in Synoptic Sayings* (Philadelphia: Fortress Press, 1975), 88ff.

47. Other proverbs Tannehill classifies as "antithetical aphorisms" are Matt. 7:18, "A good tree cannot bear bad fruit, nor can a bad tree bear good fruit"; Matt. 7:2, "For with the judgment you make you will be judged, and the measure you give will be the measure you get"; and Matt. 7:3–5 = Luke 6:41–42 (the log and the speck).

48. Sayings that Tannehill classifies as "focal instances" are Matt. 5:39–42; 5:22; 5:28; 23:8–10; Luke 12:52–53 = Matt. 10:34–36; Matt. 8:21–22; Luke 9:60, 62; Matt. 6:2, 3, 5, 6, 7; Matt. 19:24. *The Sword of His Mouth,* 72–88. I would add to the list the sayings about foot, eye, and hand: Matt. 18:8, 9; Mark 9:43.

49. Tannehill, 76.

50. James G. Williams, "Paraenesis, Excess, and Ethics: Matthew's Rhetoric in the Sermon on the Mount," *Semeia* 50 (1990): 174ff. Williams believes that Matthew uses the rhetoric of excess or hyperbole with a freer hand than Luke. Compare Matt. 5:39–42 with Luke 6:29–30, and Matt. 18:21–22 with Luke 17:4.

51. John Dominic Crossan's *Sayings Parallels: A Workbook for the Jesus Tradition* (Philadelphia: Fortress Press, 1986) contains a helpful compilation of aphorisms from the Gospels and Acts.

Chapter 7: Contemporary Proverbs

1. Gene Bluestein, *Poplore: Folk and Pop in American Culture* (Amherst, Mass.: University of Massachusetts Press, 1994), 56–57.

2. Wolfgang Mieder, *American Proverbs: A Study of Texts and Contexts* (New York: Peter Lang Publishing, 1989), 129.

3. Alan Dundes, "Folk Ideas as Units of Worldview," *Essays in Folkloristics* (Kailash Puri Meerut: Ved Prakash Vatuk. Folklore Institute, 1978), 109–10.

4. Mieder, "Different Strokes for Different Folks," *American Proverbs,* 317–24. Wolfgang Mieder, "A picture Is Worth a Thousand Words," *Proverbs Are Never Out of Season: Popular Wisdom in the Modern Age* (New York: Oxford University Press: 1993), 135–51. Wolfgang Mieder, "The Grass Is Always Greener on the Other Side of the Fence: An American Proverb of Discontent," *Proverbium* 10 (1993): 151–84.

5. These "proverbial promotions" are taken from Nigel Rees, *Dictionary of Popular Phrases* (London: Bloomsbury Publishers, 1990), and his *Why Do We Quote?* (London: Blandford Press, 1989). In both volumes they are listed by key words in alphabetical order.

6. Tim B. Rogers, "The Use of Slogans, Colloquialisms, and Proverbs in the Treatment of Substance Addiction: A Psychological Application of Proverbs," *Proverbium* 6 (1989): 108.

7. Jeffrey D. Arthurs, "Proverbs in Inspirational Literature: Sanctioning the

American Dream," *The Journal of Communication and Religion,* vol. 17, no. 2 (September 1994): 1.

8. Barbara and Wolfgang Mieder, "Tradition and Innovation: Proverbs in Advertising," in *The Wisdom of Many: Essays on the Proverb,* ed. Wolfgang Mieder (New York: Garland Publishing Co., 1981), 311.
9. Nigel Rees, *Why Do We Quote?* 226.
10. Wolfgang Mieder, "Old Wisdom in New Clothing: The Proverb in the Modern Age," *Proverbs Are Never out of Season* (New York: Oxford University Press, 1993), 65.
11. Eldridge Cleaver, "As Crinkly as Yours," *Mother Wit from the Laughing Barrel: Readings in the Interpretation of Afro-American Folklore,* compiled by Alan Dundes (New York: Garland Publishing Co., 1981), 12.
12. Rees, *Dictionary of Popular Phrases,* and *Why Do We Quote?*
13. These proverb parodies are taken from *Wise Words: Essays on the Proverb,* ed. Wolfgang Mieder (New York: Garland Publishing Co., 1994), and Jess Nierenberg, "Proverbs in Graffiti: Taunting Traditional Wisdom," 552–53.
14. The above examples of T-shirt sayings are from Alan Dundes and Carl R. Pagter, *Never Try to Teach a Pig to Sing: Still More Urban Folklore from the Paperwork Empire* (Detroit: Wayne State University Press, 1991), 67–68.
15. These examples of photocopier folklore are taken from Dundes and Pagter, *Never Try to Teach a Pig to Sing,* 69–183.
16. Rees, *Dictionary of Popular Proverbs,* 186.
17. *Wise Words,* 555.
18. Rees, *Why Do We Quote?* 78.
19. *African American Wisdom,* ed. Reginald M. McKnight (San Rafael, Calif.: New World Library, 1994), 59–61.
20. Mieder, "Proverbs of the Native Americans," *American Proverbs,* 106.
21. These proverbs are adapted from Mieder, "Afro-American Proverbs," in *American Proverbs,* 111–28 and from *African American Wisdom.*
22. Joseph Raymond, "Tensions in Proverbs: More Light on International Understanding," *The Wisdom of Many,* 301.
23. Jack L. Daniel, Geneva Smitherman-Donaldson, and Milford A. Jeremiah, "Making a Way Outa No Way: The Proverb Tradition in Black Experience" *Journal of Black Studies* 17:505.
24. Marian Wright Edelman, *The Measure of Our Success: A Letter to My Children and Yours* (New York: HarperCollins, 1993), 62.
25. Alan Dundes, "Defining Identity through Folklore," *Folklore Matters* (Knoxville, Tenn.: University of Tennessee Press, 1989), 26.
26. Rees, *Dictionary of Popular Proverbs,* 276.
27. These examples of proverbs from slavery days, as well as contemporary

sayings, are adapted from *African American Wisdom* and Mieder, *American Proverbs,* "Afro-American Proverbs," 111–23.

28. Quoted by Delores S. Williams in *Sisters in the Wilderness: The Challenge of Womanist God-Talk* (Maryknoll, N.Y.: Orbis Books, 1993), xi.

29. Nicholas C. Cooper-Lewter and Henry H. Mitchell, *Soul Theology: The Heart of American Black Culture* (Nashville: Abingdon Press, 1992), 3–4.

30. The spiritual arose as the slave's description and criticism of his environment, the key to his revolutionary sentiments and desire to fly to free territory. They express the desire for freedom, the conviction that justice would come, and the strategy of perseverance in the meantime. John Lovell, Jr., "The Social Implications of the Negro Spiritual," in *Mother Wit from the Laughing Barrel: Readings in the Interpretation of Afro-American Folklore,* compiled by Alan Dundes (New York: Garland Publishing Co., 1981), 456–60.

31. Cooper-Lewter and Mitchell, *Soul Theology,* 44.

Chapter 8: Preaching Proverbs That Create Order

1. Monica Rhor, "Giving a lift to voices and hope in an oft songless city," *The Philadelphia Inquirer,* July 29, 1995.

2. Enid LaMont Meadowcroft, *Benjamin Franklin* (New York: Scholastic Book Services, 1962), 178–79.

3. Wolfgang Mieder, "Make Hell While the Sun Shines": *Proverbial Rhetoric in Winston Churchill's* The Second World War, *Folklore* 106 (1995): 57–69.

4. Bruce K. Grant, *Korean Proverbs: Dragon Head, Snake Tail, and a Frog in a Well* (Salt Lake City: Moth House Publications, 1982), 60.

5. Dwight N. Hopkins and George Cummings, *Cut Loose Your Stammering Tongue: Black Theology in the Slave Narratives* (Maryknoll, N.Y.: Orbis Books, 1991), 49.

6. Rosa Parks and Gregory J. Reed, *Quiet Strength: The Faith, the Hope, and the Heart of a Woman Who Changed a Nation* (Grand Rapids: Zondervan Publishing House, 1995), 22.

7. From an article in the *Philadelphia Inquirer,* April 1995, "Converting the Klansman," by David O'Reilly, based on the book by Kathryn Watterson, *Not by the Sword: How the Love of a Cantor and His Family Converted a Klansman* (New York: Simon & Schuster, 1995).

8. The proverbs that follow can be paired in our preaching with New Testament texts that offer the presence of Christ as life in the present moment and the hope of eternal life as a response to the problem of righteous suffering in this life. However, it is hoped that the preacher will not feel these proverbs need to be quickly bailed out by New Testament texts, but will dwell at length on the riches of proverbial Wisdom in the context of the Proverbs collection.

9. Cat Stevens, "Wild World," from the album *Tea for the Tillerman,* PGD/A and M Records, 1970.
10. Marian Wright Edelman, *The Measure of Our Success: A Letter to My Children and Yours* (New York: HarperPerennial: 1992), 65.
11. Vivian Elaine Johnson, "Little Brother," *Daughters of Sarah,* Spring 1995 issue: "A Community of Care: Women and Aids," 41–42.

Chapter 9: Preaching Proverbs That Subvert Order

1. There are two variations on the "dueling worldviews" model: the "challenge-response" model and the "best offense is a good defense" model. The challenge-response model is based on Jesus' habit of making proverbial responses to challenges to his practices (Mark 2:19; 2:27; 9:35; Matt. 4:4; 19:24). The sermon begins with a pointed cultural challenge to an aspect of the community's faith, expressed by a contemporary reference, perhaps to the words of a public leader, a song lyric, a contemporary film, or the like. The sermon lifts up situations in which cultural wisdom and Jesus' subversive proverb compete for the community's allegiance and comes down on the side of the biblical proverb (Matt. 7:16; 15:11,14; 19:6; 19:24; 20:26–27; Mark 2:17; 3:24–25; 9:35; Luke 9:62; 18:14).

   The second, "the best defense is a good offense" is based on the prophets' strategy of using popular cultural proverbs to summarize dominant worldviews, then bringing in a corrective message from the Lord. See Jer. 8:20, 22; 12:13; 13:23; 23:28; Hos. 8:7; Zeph. 1:12; Isa. 10:15; 22:13; 37:3; 40:27. (Carole R. Fontaine, *Traditional Sayings in the Old Testament: A Contextual Study* [Sheffield: Almond Press, 1982], Appendix C, "Proverb Performance in the Old Testament Prophetic Books," 242f.) In this sermon model, the preacher sets forth the cultural proverb, then brings in another text which is not necessarily proverbial in form. For example, "Seeing is believing" is countered by Heb. 11:1f. Or "Every person has his price" could be juxtaposed with the temptation narrative.
2. Beverly Wildung Harrison, *Making the Connections* (Boston: Beacon Press, 1985), 19.
3. Robert C. Tannehill, *The Sword of His Mouth* (Society of Biblical Literature; Philadelphia: Fortress Press, 1975), 100.
4. Stephen L. Arrington, *Journey into Darkness: Nowhere to Land* (Lafayette, La.: Huntington House Publishers, 1992), 174.
5. Judith C. MacNutt, "How I Discovered Inner Healing," *Weavings: A Journal for the Christian Spiritual Life,* vol. 6, no. 4 (July-August 1991): 25–26.
6. Bruce K. Grant, *Korean Proverbs: Dragon Head, Snake Tail, and a Frog in a Well* (Salt Lake City: Moth House Publications, 1982), 7.

7. Nicholas C. Cooper-Lewter and Henry H. Mitchell, *Soul Theology: The Heart of American Black Culture.* (Nashville: Abingdon Press, 1992), 142.

8. Samuel G. Freedman, *Upon This Rock: The Miracles of a Black Church* (New York: HarperCollins Publishers, 1993), 173.

9. Stephen V. Doughty, "Glimpsing Glimpses: A Quest for Communal Discernment," *Weavings: A Journal for the Christian Spiritual Life,* 10, no. 6 (November–December 1995): 43.

10. Carlin Romano, "A Daughter of Florida," *Philadelphia Inquirer,* Feb. 19, 1995.

11. Katie Geneva Cannon, *Black Womanist Ethics* (Atlanta: Scholars Press, 1988), 4.

12. Robert Hemenway, *Zora Neale Hurston: A Literary Biography* (Urbana: University of Illinois Press, 1977), 338, quoted in Cannon, *Black Womanist Ethics,* 116.

13. Sharon D. Welch, *A Feminist Ethic of Risk* (Minneapolis: Augsburg Fortress, 1990), 15.

14. Doughty, 43–44.

15. Mary Helen Washington, Foreword to Zora Neale Hurston, *Their Eyes Were Watching God* (New York: Harper & Row, Publishers, 1990), x.

16. *Cannon,* 17.

17. "Wesley's Covenant Renewal Service," *The United Methodist Book of Worship* (Nashville: United Methodist Publishing House, 1992), 292.

Index